ENGLISH CATHEDRAL MUSIC

EDMUND H. FELLOWES

English Cathedral Music

new edition revised by
J. A. WESTRUP

236873

METHUEN & CO LTD
11 NEW FETTER LANE, LONDON EC4

First published in 1941
Second edition 1945
Third edition 1946
Fourth edition 1949
Fifth edition revised by J. A. Westrup, reset, 1969
© Methuen 1969
Printed and bound in Great Britain by
Butler and Tanner Ltd, Frome and London
SBN 416 14850 6

Distributed in the U.S.A. by
Barnes & Noble Inc

CONTENTS

FOREWORD

This revision follows the general plan of Dr Fellowes's book, though with a number of modifications in detail. Some passages have been omitted, others have been added. There has been no significant alteration of the author's opinions, except where they seemed no longer to be tenable. The cathedral music lists printed in an appendix in the original edition have been discarded, since isolated examples cannot have any statistical value. The music examples have all been revised, and most of them have been amplified or extended. Some that were in the original edition have been omitted, and new ones have been added. For advice and assistance I have to thank Professor Henry Chadwick, Mr Peter Dennison, Professor Theodore Finney and Mr David Wulstan.   J. A. W.

Oxford, 1969

PREFACE TO THE FIRST EDITION

This book has been planned to give some account of the music written for the English cathedrals and for those collegiate churches and chapels in which professional choirs have been established by ancient endowments for the performance of the daily choral services.

The term 'Cathedral Music' rather than 'Church Music' has been chosen for the title because the book deals almost exclusively with those two elaborate types of composition, the 'service' and the anthem, which are the outstanding features of cathedral usage in contrast to that of parish churches, which is ordinarily of a simpler and more congregational character. 'Church Music' is the more comprehensive term of the two; for it includes every kind of music designed for use either in cathedrals or in parish churches. It is too wide for the present purpose.

During the best part of three centuries following the introduction of the English Prayer Book little church music was performed apart from the cathedrals and collegiate chapels. The modern type of parish church choir scarcely existed either in towns or villages before the time of the Oxford Movement, and the music was limited almost entirely to metrical psalms and hymns, sometimes performed to the accompaniment of wind and stringed instruments played by local musicians.

Meanwhile during the past hundred years the music of the parish churches has developed on lines that differ in character from those of the cathedrals. Two distinct departments in church music have thus been set up. In response to the reasonable demand for simpler anthems and services, either for the canticles or for the choral Eucharist, a parish church repertory has been built up which includes much music of a high standard which is mainly modern. The longer anthems of Purcell, Boyce and Wesley, for instance, are not suitable for ordinary use in parish churches, whereas they are typical examples of the best kind of cathedral music. It is unnecessary to enlarge upon this point in relation to the settings of the canticles and the music written for the Holy Communion service.

It is reasonable that in London and other large cities a few parish churches should work upon cathedral lines as regards the musical features of their services, but these should provide the exceptions to the very general rule that the cathedral usage is out of place and unsuited to parochial worship. On the other hand, it is equally wrong that the cathedrals with their special resources, equipment, environment and traditions should draw too liberally upon the parish church repertory to the exclusion of music which can only be heard to real advantage in 'these great buildings'. The plea for brevity and popularity is utterly unworthy as an excuse for this.

The period covered here is defined in the title as 'from Edward VI to Edward VII'. The obvious starting-point seemed to be the introduction of the Prayer Book. This was not to ignore the fact that English cathedral music is far older than that. Much has recently been done to bring to light the music of the fifteenth century and earlier. The Old Hall manuscript, the Eton manuscript and the Worcester Cathedral manuscript are among the treasures which have been made accessible in modern notation by such scholars as Sir Richard Terry, the Rev. A. Ramsbotham, the Rev. Dom Anselm Hughes and Sir Ivor Atkins. These deal entirely with the old Latin rites of the Church, whereas the present book makes a dividing line in beginning with the music of the English rites.

To draw a line at which to end was less easy. It is undesirable to discuss the work of living composers, and the criticism of contemporary art in all its branches is notoriously difficult. The close of the reign of Edward VII suggested itself rather aptly. It marks an epoch in English history in many ways, more particularly because it so nearly coincides with the outbreak of war in 1914. The exclusion of living composers, for instance, involves the exclusion of Basil Harwood's music, which certainly belongs to the period dealt with in the final chapter; yet if single exceptions are made difficulties at once arise.

An appendix is added to include examples of weekly music lists or programmes that have actually been performed by some of the leading choirs. These may serve to convey some idea of the large amount of English church music that is being sung every day in these magnificent buildings throughout the country. Some older lists are added as examples of their particular period.

The author is grateful to many of his friends for suggestions and advice, more particularly to Dr H. C. Colles, Sir Sydney Nicholson, Dr H. G. Ley and Dr W. H. Harris.

E. H. FELLOWES

The Cloisters, Windsor Castle
March 1941

CHAPTER I

Music and the Reformation

There must have been some confusion in 'Quires and Places where they sing' when the changes in the church services first came into force. Much has been written on this subject from the liturgical and religious point of view; but very little attention has been drawn to the problems that must have confronted precentors, organists, choirmasters and composers, when the Latin liturgy was replaced by the Book of Common Prayer issued in the vernacular tongue.

It is not proposed here to discuss in detail ecclesiastical changes involved in the history of the English Reformation, but a brief outline may be found helpful in relation to the subject of cathedral music. It has been well stated[1] that in order to understand the Reformation it must be studied throughout the whole period from 1509 to 1662, thus carrying us, in terms of English music, from Fayrfax to Purcell. The forces which brought about the actual changes do, in fact, date at least as far back as the accession of Henry VIII in 1509, and they continued to exercise their effect until the publication of the Prayer Book in its final shape in 1662.

Even earlier than this the growth of independent thought, and with it the influence of the rising middle classes of society, was already conspicuous in the reign of Henry VII (1485–1509), having developed as an aftermath of the Wars of the Roses. Closely associated with these tendencies there came in his son's reign an ever-increasing thirst for learning, together with a wider and more liberal spirit of inquiry, which would not accept tradition unless its value could be proved under close examination. Added to this, as an inevitable corollary, came a much

[1] S. L. Ollard and G. Crosse, *A Dictionary of English Church History* (1912), p. 488.

more general study of the Scripture and a consequent demand
that an English version of the Bible should be made available
for the laity. This demand was in course of time satisfied by
Cranmer with the publication of 'the Great Bible' in 1539, from
which comes the familiar version of the Psalms which is still
retained in the Prayer Book. This led on to a feeling that the
services of the Church should be conducted 'in a tongue understanded of the people'.[1]

The crisis, as is well known, was precipitated by political
influences of quite a different character, closely affecting the
personal interests of Henry VIII. The two outstanding events
in this crisis were the suppression of the monasteries and the
introduction of the Book of Common Prayer. These were the
two events which vitally affected the history of English church
music, leading, as they did, to the creation of conspicuous types
of musical composition, entirely new and individual in style; for
the English cathedral anthem and the so-called 'service' belong
exclusively to the Anglican Church. The choral services, as
rendered daily in the English cathedrals, are unique in the
world of modern music; nothing quite like them exists on the
continent of Europe. They were the creation of English composers in the mid-sixteenth century.

The story of the Reformation does not end with the appearance of the First Prayer Book of Edward VI in 1549. In 1552
the Second Prayer Book, as the result of prolonged debate and
controversy extending over the three intervening years, superseded the First Book, which was clearly not a final measure and
was perhaps not intended to be so by its chief promoters. The
new Act of Uniformity[2] enjoined that the Second Book should
come into general use on All Saints' Day 1552. In the mean-
time John Marbeck (see p. 47) had published his *Booke of
Common Praier noted* in 1550.

The Second Prayer Book introduced many alterations; and
even those of minor importance made various details in Marbeck's musical setting out of date. It is doubtful whether the
use of Marbeck's 'noting' would have survived these changes for

[1] *Articles of Religion*, No. XXIV.
[2] 5 and 6 Ed. VI, c.i.

long; but his work was in any case swept away, together with the Second Prayer Book itself, in no more than eight months after the latter had come into use. Edward VI died in July 1553. His sister, Mary I, succeeded him on the throne, and the Latin rites were restored.

Once again the church musicians were put to some confusion. But for those that conformed to the change – and already there were several notable composers who were writing music for both the Latin and the English rites – the difficulties did not compare with those of 1549, when the need had been to find something quite new for English use. There was plenty of available music for the Marian reaction, and these conditions prevailed until the accession of Elizabeth I (1558). Nevertheless the growth of the newly founded English school of church music suffered a severe check. It is impossible to say, with so little evidence available, how all these constant upheavals, ranging over some twenty years from the dissolution of the monasteries until the accession of Elizabeth I, affected the activities of composers. But during those twenty years there had been time for new ideas to take shape and to ripen; and in the minds of men of such outstanding gifts as Tallis, Tye, Sheppard and Parsley, to mention no others, definite principles must have been forming and coming to maturity; so that when once more the English rites came into use under Elizabeth I, the necessary experience had been gained, and the problems could be faced, as indeed they were, with brilliant success. But the Marian gap of five years accounts for much in reference to the marked advance shown by comparing the English compositions of the period of the First Prayer Book and those of early Elizabethan days. Moreover, the influence of the Italian school, in both secular and church music, during these two decades must not be overlooked. Italian music itself had progressed far during this same period, and its influence on the Elizabethan composers contributed much to their development, even though it did not impair the national and independent characteristics of their style.

A fresh Act of Uniformity was passed in April 1559[1] which

---

[1] I Eliz., c.2.

authorized a further revision of the Prayer Book; it specified the
Feast of St John the Baptist as the day on which it was to come
into use. This revision in no way concerns the musical details of
the service. But the period of controversy between rival religious partisans within the Anglican Communion extended
after this into the seventeenth century. Further alterations in
the Prayer Book were made in 1604 following the accession of
James I; but these were of minor importance. His reign and
that of Charles I were notable for the rivalry between extreme
Protestant and Calvinistic teaching on the one side, and that
of the conservative churchmen, as championed by Bishop
Andrewes and Archbishop Laud, on the other.

The Civil War, the execution of Charles I and the period of
the Commonwealth followed. During this period the Puritan
party gained and held the ascendancy, and the English Church
itself went near to complete extinction. This was another
tremendous blow to English church music, still only in its
adolescence and following, as it did, the decay of the great
school of Elizabethan composition. The cathedrals were closed
by order of Parliament; the clergy and choirs were dismissed;
organs were mutilated and music-books destroyed. This whole-
sale destruction of music-books has caused the irretrievable loss
of an unknown quantity of anthems and services composed by
Tudor musicians.

For some fifteen years church music, apart from the singing
of metrical psalms, was non-existent in England. Secular music,
both vocal and instrumental, escaped such a fate. With the
Restoration of Charles II in 1660 came the resumption of full
choral services. They were restored in the cathedrals and collegiate chapels, never to be interrupted again from that day to
this. The church musicians had no easy task, after fifteen years
or more of silence, in reviving the musical features in their full
glory. The organists and choirmasters had to lay entirely new
foundations upon which to rebuild the choirs, and also to
collect and train the boys.

It was in May 1662 that the Restoration Act of Uniformity
was finally passed. Deans and chapters of every cathedral and
collegiate church were ordered to obtain an official copy of

the Prayer Book, as finally sanctioned by that Act, before the following Christmas Day. The Prayer Book of 1662 is the Prayer Book as we know it today; and its issue may truly be said to mark the actual completion of the Reformation move-ment, dating back in its origin to the accession of Henry VIII in 1509.

In this extended period of more than a century and a half the two outstanding events that have special bearing upon the history of English church music are, as has already been stated, the suppression of the monasteries and the issue of the Prayer Book in 1549. They need therefore to be considered here at further length.

First, the suppression of the monasteries. This was not the work of a single day, nor the result of a single order or decree. In 1535 Thomas Cromwell, in addition to the other high positions in the state which he held, was appointed Vicar-General in causes ecclesiastical for the purpose of carrying out the Act of Supremacy.[1] It was in the summer of that same year that Sir Thomas More suffered martyrdom on Tower Hill, largely through the instrumentality of Cromwell; several execu-tions of monks had already taken place. Commissioners were appointed to visit and collect information about the monas-teries, and in due course their report, reinforced by an Act of Parliament, resulted in all the minor monasteries, abbeys and priories under the value of £200 per annum being condemned. That was in 1536. The greed of the king, as well as many of his courtiers who shared in the plunder, was encouraged by this initial success, and it soon became clear that the larger re-ligious houses would suffer a similar fate. In the years 1538 and 1539 almost the whole of the work of suppression and expro-priation was completed. In the autumn of 1539 the magnificent Benedictine abbeys of Reading, Glastonbury and Colchester, which were among the last survivors, were surrendered and destroyed, and their abbots summarily executed.

Westminster Abbey itself surrendered on 16 January 1540. It was at first re-founded by Henry VIII as a cathedral church, the abbot becoming dean in association with six canons and six

[1] 26 Hen. VIII, c.i.

minor canons. Subsequently in 1550 the bishopric was surrendered and suppressed, and the Abbey church united to the see of London. In 1560 Elizabeth I re-founded the collegiate church as a 'Royal Peculiar', staffed by a dean and twelve prebendaries.

Westminster Abbey was not alone among the monastic establishments that were re-founded by Henry VIII as cathedral churches. Those that were so reconstituted came to be known as cathedrals of the new foundation, in contrast to the establishments of the old foundation which from medieval times had remained under the direction of secular clergy (i.e. those who were not members of a religious order). These latter continued their existence unchanged in the troubled period of Henry's reign. The new foundation cathedrals include Canterbury, Winchester, Durham, Oxford, Chester, Gloucester, Worcester, Rochester, Norwich, Ely, Peterborough and Carlisle.

The suppression of the monasteries struck a very severe blow at English church music. In a large proportion of them the daily services were fully choral, and choirs of men and boys were provided for by their endowments and statutes. Song-schools were in consequence very numerous throughout the country, and those that were not incorporated in the new foundations were ruthlessly swept away by Thomas Cromwell and his men when the monasteries perished. Many hundreds of singing-men were deprived of their position and thrown on to their own resources to earn a livelihood as best they could. The fate of Waltham Abbey will serve as an illustration of what occurred in similar establishments throughout England. An inventory taken at the time of its suppression and dated 24 March, 31 Henry VIII,[1] gives a list of the names of some seventy persons who received a small gratuity on being deprived of their office. This list includes the name of Thomas Tallis (see p. 45). Five choristers were mentioned in the inventory, and apparently about twelve singing-men, though the exact number cannot be precisely ascertained from the original document. The inventory also shows that there was 'a lytell payre of organes' in the Lady Chapel, and that in the choir was 'a great larg payre of

---

[1] P.R.O., Exchequer K.R., Church goods 11/24.

organs' and 'also a lesser payr'. Assuming, at a conservative
estimate, that out of a total of some six hundred monastic
establishments suppressed, considerably more than two hundred
were equipped on anything like the same scale as at Waltham
Abbey, it will be recognized that a very large number of
singing-men, and a corresponding number of trained musicians
as their choirmasters, must have been thrown out of employment. Tallis secured employment at Canterbury, and soon
afterwards in the Chapel Royal. But a great number of musicians
must have been less fortunate.

The first Act of Uniformity was passed on 21 January 1549;
it ordered that 'the Book of Common Prayer and none other'
was to be used on and after the Feast of Pentecost, which fell
on 9 June that year. This meant that the musical settings of the
Mass, the motets, and all other sacred music wedded to the
Latin language, were completely ruled out. It was necessary
at once to provide music for the Anglican use in the cathedrals and similar establishments; this included the Versicles
and Responses, the Psalms, the Litany, the canticles (both for
Mattins and Evensong), as well as anthems. As regards the
replacement of the Latin Mass the immediate need was at first
supplied with some existing English settings of the whole Office
of the Holy Communion, including *Sanctus*, *Benedictus*, *Agnus Dei*
and *Gloria in excelsis*. But on this subject more will be said
later (see p. 36).

By Whitsuntide 1549 the demand for musical services in
English had already to some small extent been anticipated.
That the substitution of the English language in place of Latin
in the church services had been spreading with considerable
force is demonstrated, as will be shown presently, by the con-
tents of certain manuscripts. Church musicians were not be-
hindhand in seeing what was coming. A form of Litany with
English words had actually come into existence before the close
of the fifteenth century. In 1544 Cranmer's revision was published by Thomas Berthelet almost exactly in its present form,
with each clause adapted to the music of the traditional Latin
plainsong. Another of the earlier steps towards the use of English
was taken when the Primer of Henry VIII was issued in 1545.

Musical services on a cathedral scale were being performed in English for some time before the passing of the Act of Uniformity. Among the early manuscripts is a remarkable set of three part-books now in the Bodleian Library at Oxford.[1] The date usually assigned to them is 1546–7. They are known as the 'Wanley' part-books for the reason that at one time they were owned by the famous librarian Humfrey Wanley, who presented them to the Bodleian Library early in the eighteenth century. Unfortunately the tenor part-book is missing: the set should consist of four part-books to make it complete. The missing book had without doubt disappeared before Wanley's time. But although this is to be deplored on the ground that the text of all the music in this set of books is incomplete, yet it in no way detracts from their historical interest and importance. These books include between eighty and ninety musical compositions set to English words, including the morning and evening canticles, two harmonized settings of the plainsong of the Litany, a large number of anthems, and, what is still more remarkable, ten English settings of the Office for the Holy Communion, complete with *Kyrie*, *Credo*, *Gloria in excelsis*, *Sanctus*, *Benedictus* and *Agnus Dei*.

---

[1] Mus. Sch. e. 420–2.

The Tradition

The change brought about by the substitution of English for Latin throughout the country[1] had the effect of laying the foundation stone of a new structure. English church music, and more particularly cathedral music, as we know it today, has its origin in the Reformation.

The national character of the English choral service is a subject of the highest importance to churchmen, and especially to church musicians, but it should also appeal in the strongest terms even to those English musicians whose interests may be mainly concerned with secular music. The English anthem is a musical form that is distinctively and exclusively national; so too is the traditional form upon which the 'services', or musical settings of the canticles, are constructed, not to mention the Anglican method of chanting the psalms. During the 400 years that have elapsed since the Prayer Book was first introduced, a wonderful repertory of this class of music has been built up by successive generations of English composers. It is true that in the eighteenth and nineteenth centuries the standard both of composition and of performance was allowed to degenerate to a deplorable extent; and it is significant that this lapse coincided closely with the decay of spiritual and religious life in the Church of England. But even so an unbroken chain, though a slender one at times, unites modern church musicians with those of the Tudor and Restoration periods. They hold the same ideals in their effort to provide music worthy of its supreme purpose, that of contributing something of beauty to the act of worship.

[1] Latin was allowed, and is still allowed to be used where it is understood – in college chapels at the universities and at Winchester and Eton, and also in Convocation.

The English have always had a strong instinct for choral music. This instinct has in the past had a very powerful influence upon the actual rendering of the choral services. It was also conspicuous at a period even earlier than the Reformation. There has never been lacking a plentiful supply of men and boys well qualified for the skilled task of singing music which is often of an elaborate and difficult character. Those who, with a very limited allowance of time, have had the practical experience of teaching boys to sing with the full choir two anthems, four canticles and the psalms every weekday, as well as heavier work still on Sundays, and at the same time to add fresh music to the repertory, are unanimous in expressing their amazement at the quickness with which the boys learn their work.

It is sometimes argued that choristers have to give so much time to their cathedral work that their ordinary education must suffer. It is true that Mattins, Evensong and at least one choir-practice may occupy together about two hours and a half daily. It is true also that something in their school curriculum must be sacrificed to permit this. Nevertheless there are compensations which outweigh these disadvantages. A chorister necessarily cultivates a power of concentration which nothing else could give him at that age. This acquired power is invaluable to him for life, and it enables him soon to outstrip other boys in later school-days even though he may at first be behind them. Added to this, he cultivates a taste for beautiful English, absorbed quite subconsciously and without effort, by chanting the psalms and hearing the language of the Bible and Prayer Book twice a day. In the course of four years or more in the choir he gets to know the psalms practically by heart. There could be no more effective training than this for writing good English and acquiring an appreciation of fine literature. It is unnecessary here to emphasize the value of the religious experience, which so many former choristers prize greatly in later life.

The training provided by the existence of endowed choirs has also made them the nurseries of musical composition. Few notable English musicians could be named from the sixteenth century to the close of the nineteenth who did not begin their careers as choristers in the Chapel Royal, or in some cathedral or college choir. Examples are Byrd, Gibbons, Purcell, Blow, Greene, Boyce, S. S. Wesley, Stainer and Sullivan.

The value and importance of the cathedral service as a national heritage is not always sufficiently understood – least of all by those members of the capitular bodies of certain cathedrals who aim at curtailing and discontinuing some of the daily choral services on the plea that they deprive them personally of an extra half-hour or so for their own studies; they presume to argue that this outweighs the additional dignity which fine music, reverently and adequately rendered, must inevitably lend to the recital of the daily offices.

The full choral service justly claims to be an act of worship. The value of worship in the Christian economy is sometimes forgotten in the present age of turmoil, when it is apt to be obscured by the overwhelming calls of pastoral and social activities. These are not to be minimized; but worship must also be given its proper place. In the past this principle has always stood; and it is conspicuous in all forms of religious observance. Christian worship, tracing its origin, as it does, to some of the ceremonial features of ancient Jewish ritual, has always made great use of music and singing as a means of enhancing its dignity and its beauty. In the Mosaic scheme the value of worship, beautified by music, was recognized in the special work assigned to the *Nethinim* as a branch of the Levitical priesthood.

It is in this ancient tradition that the modern cathedral service stands. What would be the value of these glorious buildings with their magnificent architectural and decorative features if no services were held in them? It is not 'the altar' but 'the gift upon the altar' that counts. Westminster Abbey or Canterbury Cathedral would be no more than interesting museums without the services held in them daily. And it must be the most beautiful form of service possible, adorned with everything that art can lend it to make it a worthy offering to Almighty God. To carry out this noble purpose in no way excludes the numberless ways in which the cathedral church of a diocese may also be employed for pastoral work, for popular 'nave services', and in several other directions. Yet the first and main purpose of these foundations is embodied in the daily choral services, and that purpose must not be set aside for any cause.

Complaint is sometimes made that the cost of maintaining a cathedral type of service is too heavy to justify it, including, as it does, the stipends of the minor canons, the organist and the lay clerks, together with a choir-school, not to mention the upkeep of the organ and the cost of music. Could not these funds be better employed in missionary work, or to support pastoral work in impoverished town-parishes? Such a view is similar to the protest made to Christ when 'the box of ointment of spikenard, very precious' was used by a poor sinner to anoint his feet – an act of worship. With indignation at such apparent waste it was argued that 'this ointment might have been sold for much and given to the poor'. The protest seemed reasonable, but it was not. Christ gave his unqualified approval in a remarkable way, adding that the story of this incident was to be an undying one; that 'what this woman hath done shall be told for a memorial of her'. He intended it to be symbolical. He was proclaiming for all time the spiritual value of worship in terms of costly offering.

CHAPTER 3

Music and the Anglican Services

The term 'cathedral service', as used here, denotes one that is sung by an endowed and professional choir, such as is found in the principal diocesan cathedrals of the United Kingdom and Ireland, together with the Chapel Royal, Westminster Abbey and St George's Chapel, Windsor, in all of which there is an unbroken tradition going back to the sixteenth century as regards the English Use, and to medieval times with the older Latin rites. Added to these establishments are the college chapels at the older universities, and certain minster and abbey churches, in which full choral services have continued to be maintained on a cathedral scale from early days. The three services in the Book of Common Prayer with which a cathedral choir is mainly concerned are Mattins, Evensong and the Office of the Holy Communion. From beginning to end these services are, or should be, sung in accordance with the ancient choral rules of the Church of England, founded, as these were, upon the older Latin use in this country before the Reformation.

The English form of Mattins was first set out in the Prayer Book of 1549. As regards the opportunities for musical treatment, it does not differ greatly from what is in use today. The opening section of Mattins did not yet exist. The service was begun by the priest with the Lord's Prayer, followed by 'O Lorde, open thou my lippes', and it ended with the third collect.

The Second Prayer Book,[1] which came into use on All Saints' Day 1552, added the opening section to Mattins, that is to say, the Sentences, the Exhortation, the Confession and Absolution; and the only other change of any consequence affecting the

---

[1] Both the First and the Second Prayer Books were published in Everyman's Library (1910), with an introduction by the Bishop of Gloucester.

music was the insertion of *Jubilate* as an alternative to *Benedictus*. This book was in use for little more than eight months before the English services were discontinued under the Marian reaction, when the Latin rites were restored. No alterations in Mattins that concern musicians were made in the Elizabethan version of the Prayer Book issued in 1559. The final prayers after the third collect were not added until 1662.

The development of Evensong closely followed that of Mattins, except that the opening portion before the first Lord's Prayer was not added in 1552 as it was to Mattins: this was inserted in 1662. The canticles *Cantate Domino* and *Deus misereatur* were added in 1552 as alternatives to *Magnificat* and *Nunc dimittis*. In the reign of Elizabeth I Mattins and Evensong were sung very much as they are now as regards their musical plan. One difference was the practice of singing *Venite* to a full setting like the other canticles. The practice prevailed throughout the latter part of the sixteenth century and possibly until the Civil War, since when *Venite* has always been sung to a chant.

From early times all the prayers, including the opening portion of the service and the final prayers, when they were added, were intoned by the priest on a definite note, and the Confession, the Lord's Prayer (both times) and the Creed were intoned by the choir 'after [i.e. led by] the minister'. The *Preces, Versicles and Responses* were at first probably sung to Marbeck's melodies (see p. 22) unharmonized; the more elaborate style of harmony with which they were set seems to belong to the Elizabethan period. The rubric both in 1549 and 1552 orders that 'in such places where they doe syng', there shall be the lessons be 'songe in a playne tune'. This followed the old Latin practice, and inflexions were probably introduced in the same manner as in the Epistle and Gospel.

By what method the psalms were chanted when the Prayer Book first appeared is a question which has never yet been answered with any certainty. Marbeck printed an adaptation of the plainsong tone 8, 1st ending for the first verse of *Venite* at Mattins and for the first verse of Psalm 6 ('O Lord, rebuke me not') at Evensong, adding in each case: 'And so forth wyth the rest of the Psalmes, as they be appoynted.' This is in contrast to the canticles, where the music is printed for each verse. To have done this with the complete psalter would obviously have been impossible. For lack of any other evidence it must remain uncertain whether in fact the psalms were sung to Marbeck's psalm-tones. If they were, it is likely that the practice was discontinued when his book fell into disuse, as did other experiments during the reign of Mary I, not to be revived with the Elizabethan return to the English rite.

It is not impossible that in Elizabethan times the daily psalms were sometimes sung to metrical versions of the words – a practice that has survived continuously in the Presbyterian churches. In a memorandum dated 14 February 1565,[1] concerning the 'Varieties in Service and the Administration used', Grindal, when Bishop of London, stated that 'some kepe precysely ye ord^r of ye booke oth^rs intermedle Psal: in meter'. The Puritan influence in England was considerably stronger from 1558 onwards than it had been even in 1552; and it is noteworthy that several metrical versions of the entire psalter had appeared in print before the end of the sixteenth century. The metrical psalms, however, were not originally intended for such use. In 1562 Horne, Bishop of Winchester, ordered[2] that the cathedral choir were to sing one of the metrical psalms at the discretion of the precentor both before and after the sermon, and to have in readiness for this purpose books of psalms set forth in English metre, to be provided at the costs of the church. The Anglican chant, even in its single form, did not come into general use as early as this, but the harmonized versions of the Gregorian melodies as printed by Thomas Morley[3] may already have been in use in Elizabeth's reign, as they certainly were in the seventeenth century up to the time of the Restoration. A curious example of a Latin psalm-tone adapted to metrical psalms occurs in an anonymous psalter published in 1549.[4] The book

[1] British Museum, Lansdowne 8, fo. 16.
[2] *Visitation Articles and Injunctions of the Period of the Reformation*, ed. W. H. Frere, iii, p. 138.
[3] *A Plaine and Easie Introduction to Practicall Musicke*, p. 147 (modern edition by R. A. Harman, p. 250).
[4] See *Grove's Dictionary of Music* (5th ed.), vi, p. 958. There is a copy of the psalter in the library of Brasenose College, Oxford.

includes a single tune to which all the psalms can be sung. The setting is a four-part harmonization of tone 7, 1st ending, with the plainsong in the tenor:

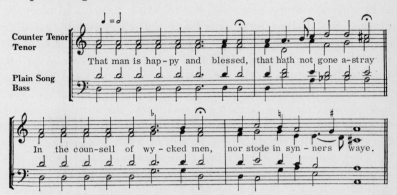

Another method of singing the psalms in Elizabethan times was designed primarily for the great church festivals. Several composers, for example Tallis, Parsons and Byrd, and at a rather later date Gibbons, Tomkins and Hooper, wrote settings for the Proper Psalms for Christmas, Easter Day, Ascension Day and Whit-Sunday. In principle and design they are not unlike the modern Anglican chant, and directions are given for antiphonal treatment by the *decani* and *cantoris* sides of the choir. The main melodic material usually recurs in every verse, and in certain settings every two verses, but the phrases in both cases are extended or shortened in accordance with the varying number of words in each individual verse. Only the first few verses of any psalm were fitted to the music, and the elaborate nature of the structure points to the conclusion that the remaining verses were omitted in performance. In the Caroline partbooks at Peterhouse, Cambridge, these settings are called *psalmi festivales*. This method of chanting represents in English use the old Latin practice of singing *salmi concertati* on special occasions such as the great festivals. The following verses from Byrd's setting of Psalm 47 (for Ascension Day)[1] will serve to illustrate the design of these festival chants:

[1] *Tudor Church Music*, ii, p. 5.

The fifth verse, with its special reference to this festival, is slightly elaborated:

The existence of this special usage argues that a simpler form was employed for ordinary occasions and for daily use.

The earliest Anglican chants may owe their origin partly to these *psalmi festivales,* but perhaps more directly to the harmonization of the eight Gregorian tones. Again, certain old melodies very closely foreshadowed the Anglican chant. For instance, the French tune known as 'Old 124th',[1] from its association with the metrical version of Psalm 124, can be cut up into single and double Anglican chants without any alteration whatever:

Whatever its actual origin may have been, the single Anglican chant probably dates from early in the seventeenth century, but the double chant did not come into general use until after the Restoration. The single chants assigned in modern collections

---

[1] First printed in the Genevan Psalter of 1551. The version given here is from the Anglo-Genevan Psalter of 1558 (bar-lines editorial).

to Elizabethan composers are adaptations from other works. There are no genuine Anglican chants known to have been written as such by Tallis, Farrant, Byrd or Orlando Gibbons, for example.

No consideration of the harmonized settings of the Responses and Litany can be entered upon satisfactorily without some reference to the whole subject of intoning. This subject was dealt with in a very full and authoritative manner by John Jebb in the prefaces to his two volumes of *The Choral Responses and Litanies of the United Church of England and Ireland* (1847, 1857), as well as in a treatise entitled *The Choral Service of the United Church of England and Ireland*, published in 1843. Though written more than a century ago most of Jebb's statements and arguments are in no sense out of date today. Jebb was careful to explain that his purpose was not to advance theories of his own but only to record what has been the actual practice of the English Church. In writing this he was referring solely to the cathedral type of service; it was no part of his plan to promote congregational or parochial chanting in ordinary churches:

> [The] choral recitation [of the Responses] forms . . . an integral part of the worship peculiar to our Cathedrals, and Collegiate Churches and Chapels. . . . In all *Exhortations*, *Sentences*, and *Absolutions*, and in all those *Collects* or *Prayers* which are pronounced by the Minister alone, and are responded to by *Amen*, it is the choral rule of the Church of *England* to use one unvaried musical tone.

After this Jebb goes on to deal at considerable length with the meaning of the phrase 'said or sung' in the rubrics. He states that the word 'say' does not exclude a musical tone, but refers merely to what is simply recited in contradistinction to a regular chant or elaborate musical setting. In the 1549 Prayer Book one of the rubrics in the Communion Service runs: '*Then shall the priest saye* The peace of the Lorde be always with you. *The Clerkes* And with thy spirite.' Jebb argues that in this passage the word '*saye*' can only mean 'intone'. Again, the Nicene Creed, for example, is ordered by the rubric to be 'sung or said'; Jebb explains that if it be recited on a monotone, even with a cadence for the *Amen*, this would not properly be called

'singing', it would be 'saying' in accordance with the ancient
rules of the Church. He insists also, and quite rightly, that the
harmonized cadence for an *Amen* is the final inflexion and a
definite part of the chant to which any prayer has been intoned.
It is entirely incorrect for a choir to sing an *Amen* at the conclusion of a prayer that has been offered in a spoken voice.

Jebb would have had no sympathy with the practice of reading the opening section of Mattins and Evensong, and the
prayers that follow the anthem, in the spoken voice. There are
grave disadvantages in the use of the spoken voice instead of
intoning these parts of the service in a cathedral. First, the
spoken voice does not carry far in a large resonant building, and
it is difficult to distinguish even the familiar words from a short
distance away, though admittedly the use of a microphone
eliminates this difficulty. The recital of the prayers, by any
method, differs fundamentally from oratory. The voice cannot
be raised to anything like the same extent as in making a
speech or in preaching, nor is there the same scope for variety of
inflexion. The rubric referring to the lessons in the Prayer Book,
both in 1549 and 1552, confirms this point. It was 'to thende
[i.e. the end] the people may the better heare' that it was
enjoined that 'in such places where they doe syng, there shall
the lessons be songe in a playne tune after the maner of distincte
readyng: and lykewyse the Epistle and Gospell'.

Secondly, the impersonal character of the intoning voice has
a very definite value (in the control of an intelligent chanter),
as compared with the individual inflexions which a reader inevitably introduces when using the spoken voice, however well
he performs his task. Francis Close, a former Dean of Carlisle,
writing at a time when the subject of Cathedral music was
being keenly debated, stated that as a result of regular attendance at the daily choral services he had experienced a growing
appreciation of the continuous monotone in which the prayers
were uttered.[1] As the alternative to hearing the prayers spoken
'with varieties of emphasis and enunciation', the musical style
of recitation was, in his opinion, greatly preferable. It was noteworthy that Close was a strong Evangelical. One more comment

[1] *Thoughts on the Daily Choral Services* (1865), p. 110.

on this point. In a very resonant building the effect produced by a body of people mumbling the Confession, the Lord's Prayer or the Creed in their spoken voices at various pitches, with no syllables or inflexions coinciding, is cacophonous in the extreme; and the spoken, or rather murmured, *Amens* sound like a half-stifled 'umm'. Such an effect cannot seriously be regarded as dignified in association with the other features of a cathedral service; it can have no relation to the idea of beauty in worship, and, moreover, it is without doubt contrary to the choral rule of the English Church which, as Jebb pointed out, has now prevailed for nearly 400 years.

There can be little doubt that in cathedral choirs the direction to intone the lessons was observed, with the traditional inflexions inherited from the Latin practice. For this purpose in many places the duty of reading the lessons was assigned, not to a canon but to a minor canon, or priest vicar, or in some instances to a lay-clerk, as being people qualified on musical grounds to perform a duty requiring special skill. It was for similar reasons that lay members of the Chapel Royal held the appointment of 'pisteler' (i.e. epistoler). It may be doubted whether the lessons continued to be intoned in many places after the period of the Commonwealth, but there is a tradition that the practice was maintained at Canterbury and Lincoln longer than elsewhere.

The Versicles and Responses and the Litany may now be considered. In Mattins and Evensong there are two groups of versicles which take the form of short petitions followed by responses. Each group is preceded by the *Lord's Prayer* and leads up to what follows immediately.

The first of these groups has been called the *Sursum corda* of the daily service,[1] and, as such, it leads to the psalms, preceded at Mattins by *Venite*. It begins with *O Lord, open thou our lips*, and the group was known as the *Preces*. Many of the Elizabethans set these to music, notably Tallis, Byrd, Morley, Gibbons and Tomkins. In the Prayer Books of 1549 and 1552 the *Gloria Patri* in this group was assigned in its entirety to the priest, but the composers usually set it to full harmony to be sung by

[1] J. H. Blunt, *The Annotated Book of Common Prayer*, p. 150.

C

the choir. The response to the *Gloria* was *Praise ye the Lord*. In the Latin Office (according to the Sarum Use) the *Gloria Patri* is intoned on a single note, with inflexions at 'Sancto', 'semper' and 'Amen': it is followed by a brief cadence on 'Alleluia'. Marbeck adapted this formula to the English text, as a comparison of the Sarum 'Alleluia'[1] with his setting of 'Praise ye the Lord'[2] will show:

(a) Al - le - lu - ya.   (b) Prayse ye the lorde.

When the Preces and Responses took their final shape in 1662 the final response was itself divided into a versicle and a response; *Praise ye the Lord* became a versicle with the response *The Lord's Name be praised*.

The second group of versicles at Mattins and Evensong is that which leads up to the three collects. This group was set to music by far fewer Elizabethan composers. The best-known of these harmonized settings is that by Tallis; but Byrd, Morley and Tomkins, among others, also set them. Almost all these settings are based on Marbeck, who follows a simple principle as regards the final inflexion; that is to say, if the final word is a monosyllable the melody falls a minor third and rises again by a tone; if the final word has more than one syllable the melody falls a minor third on the last syllable. A single exception to this rule is found in the original edition of Marbeck's book, where the final versicle is printed:

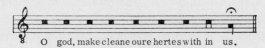

O   god, make cleane oure hertes with in   us.

It is generally admitted that this must be a printer's error which escaped correction.

---

[1] *Antiphonale Sarisburiense*, ed. W. H. Frere (1901–24), pl. a.
[2] The same setting is given by E[dward] L[owe], *A Short Direction for the Performance of Cathedrall Service* (1661), p. 5. Marbeck's notation follows a scheme peculiar to himself. He calls the first note in the above example a 'square note' and defines it as a semibreve. The second note is a 'strene [i.e. strain] note', defined as a breve. The last note is a 'close, and is only used at yᵉ end of a verse'.

The melody was usually assigned to the tenor in the early harmonizations, but in the ferial use (i.e. on days other than festivals) it is given to the treble. Some of the examples of choral responses printed by Jebb,[1] as being the special 'use' of certain cathedrals, are eighteenth-century developments of a somewhat debased character: they are constructed without due regard to traditional principles.

The so-called Lesser Litany, which in the Second Prayer Book[2] immediately precedes the second recitation of the *Lord's Prayer*, consists of three petitions addressed to the three persons of the Trinity:

> Lord, ⎫
> Christ, ⎬ have mercy upon us.
> Lord, ⎭

Tallis, Byrd, Morley and others provided harmonizations of the melody. The versicles and responses that occur in the occasional services of the Prayer Book do not call for comment.

The Litany, except for a few trifling modifications in certain suffrages, appeared exactly in its present form in 1544. It was the work of Archbishop Cranmer, who also adapted the plain-song melody of the Latin text to the English use. This is the plainsong which has ever since been associated with the English Litany in various harmonized settings. Cranmer's Litany was included in a publication issued by Thomas Berthelet on 27 May 1544, entitled 'An exhortation unto prayer, thoughte mete by the kinges maiestie, and his clergy, to be read to the people in every church afore processyons. Also a Letanie with suffrages to be said or song in the tyme of the said processyons.'[3] Other editions of this were issued on 16 June and 12 October of the same year.[4] The text of the Litany in these publications was accompanied by Cranmer's plainsong notation. In an interleaved copy of Maunsell's *Catalogue of English Books* (1595), now in the Cambridge University Library, it was stated that there was published by Richard Grafton on 26 June 1544 'The letany

---

[1] *Choral Responses and Litanies.*
[2] In the First Prayer Book it precedes the Creed.
[3] Facsimile edition by J. Eric Hunt (1939).
[4] F. E. Brightman, *The English Rite* (1915), i, p. lx.

in five parts accordyng to the notes used in the Kynges Maies-
ties Chapel'.[1] But no trace of this seems to have been discovered.

It was at this time that Henry VIII and Cranmer were pro-
jecting a complete English Processional on the lines of the
Latin *Processionale*. On 7 October 1545 Cranmer wrote to the
king in the following terms:[2]

> It may please Your Majestie to be advertised, that, according
> to Your Highnes commaundemente . . . I have translated into
> the Englishe tongue, so well as I coulde in so shorte a tyme,
> certeyne processions, to be used apon festivall daies, yf after due
> correction and amendemente of the same, Your Highness shall
> thinke it so conveniente. In whiche translacion . . . I was con-
> strayned to use more than the libertie of a translator; for in some
> processions, I have altered divers wourdes; in some, I have added
> parte; in some, taken parte awaie; some I have lefte oute hole; . . .
> and some procession I have added hole, bycause I thought I hadd
> better matter for the purpose, than was the procession in Latten;
> . . . and after Your Highnes hath corrected yt, yf Your Grace
> commande some devoute and solempne note to be made there-
> unto (as is to the procession, which Your Majestie hath alredie
> setfurth in Englishe), I truste it woll moche excitate and stirre the
> hartes of all men unto devotion and godlynes; but, in myn
> opinion, the songe that shalbe made thereunto wolde not be full
> of notes, but, as nere as may be, for every sillable, a note; so that
> it may be songe distinctly and devoutly, as be in the Matens and
> Evensong, Venite, the Hymnes, Te Deum, Benedictus, Magnificat,
> Nunc dimittis, and all the Psalmes and Versicles, and in the
> Masse, Gloria in excelsis, Gloria Patri, the Crede, the Preface,
> the Pater noster, and some of the Sanctus and Agnus. As con-
> cernyng the Salve festa dies,[3] the Latten note (as I think) is
> sobre and distincte enoughe; wherfore I have travailid to make
> the versis in Englishe, and have put the Latten note unto the
> same. Nevertheless thei, that be connyng in syngyng, can make a
> moche more solempne note therto. I make them only for a profe,
> to see howe Englishe wolde do in songe. But by cause myn
> Englishe versis lacke the grace and facilitie, that I wolde wishe
> they hadd, Your Majestie may cause some other to make theym
> againe, that can do the same in more pleasante English and
> phrase.

[1] J. Ames, *Typographical Antiquities*, ed. W. Herbert (1785), i, p. 519.
[2] *State Papers*, i (1830), p. 760.
[3] A Latin processional, known in English as 'Hail, festal day'.

Cranmer makes three main points: (1) that he has adapted a number of Latin processions and in one case (or some cases – the text is not clear) has written entirely new words; (2) that these texts should be set to syllabic chants similar to those used for the canticles, psalms, etc.; (3) that he thinks the existing melody for *Salve festa dies* will do very well for his English version.

The project of producing an English Processional advanced no further, and the Litany alone remains that would have been included in it. It is incorrect, however, to describe the Litany as *the* Procession. The Royal Injunctions issued for Lincoln Minster in 1548 (§26) order that it should be sung in the middle of the choir on Sundays, Wednesdays and Fridays.[1] It was by exception that it was sung in procession – for example, at Rogationtide.

It was the form and ceremonial of the English rite of the Holy Communion that caused the most bitter controversy throughout the whole period of the Reformation. Here we are concerned mainly with the musical features of this service. The rubric of the 1549 Prayer Book enjoins that after the *Lord's Prayer*, the collect and a psalm, 'said' by the priest for the introit,

> *the Priest shall saye, or els the Clerkes shal syng,*
> iii Lorde have mercie upon us, &c.
> *Then the Priest standyng at Goddes borde shall begin,*
> Glory be to God on high.
> *The Clerkes.* And in yearth peace, &c.

After the announcement of the Gospel

> *The Clearkes and people shall aunswere,*
> Glory be to thee, O Lorde.
> *After the Gospel ended, the Priest shall begin,*
> I beleve in one God.
> *The clerkes shall syng the rest.*

Then came the sermon, or one of the long exhortations still included in the Prayer Book.

---

[1] *Statutes of Lincoln Cathedral*, ed. H. Bradshaw and C. Wordsworth, iii (1897), p. 593.

*Then shall folowe for the Offertory, one or mo, of these Sentences of holy
scripture, to bee song whiles the people doo offer. . . .*
    Let your light so shine before men, &c.
*Where there be Clerkes, thei shall syng one, or many of the sentences above
written, accordyng to the length and shortnesse of the tyme, that the people
be offeryng.*
Then the Priest shall saye
    The Lorde be with you.
Aunswere. And with thy spirite.
Priest. Lift up your heartes.

And so on in the familiar words still in use, until the *Sanctus*:

    Holy, holy, holy, Lorde God of Hostes: heaven and earth are
full of thy glory: Osanna in the highest. Blessed is he that commeth
in the name of the Lorde: Glory to thee, O lorde in the highest.
This the Clerkes shall also syng.

This was followed by the prayer 'for the whole state of Christes
churche'.

The order of the service after this differs considerably from
the present arrangement. The choir was next concerned with
Agnus Dei:

In the Communion tyme the Clarkes shall syng,
    ii. O lambe of god, &c.,

after which,

*beginning so soone as the Prieste doeth receyve the holy Communion,
and when the Communion is ended, then shall the Clerkes syng the post
Communion.*
    *Sentences of holy Scriptures, to be sayd or song every daye one, after the
holy Communion, called the post Communion.*
    If any man will folowe me, &c.

Settings of all these sentences are provided in Marbeck's book.

In 1552 many changes were made, and the arrangement of
the service was much the same as it is now. The Ten Commandments, with the responses to them, replaced the threefold
form of *Kyrie eleison. Gloria in excelsis* was moved from the beginning to its present place, and *Benedictus, Agnus Dei* and the post-
Communions disappeared.

The portions available for setting to music in a free style are the *Kyrie, Credo, Offertory Sentences, Sanctus* and *Gloria in excelsis*. To these should be added *Benedictus* and *Agnus Dei*, which are now again in general use. *Sursum corda* ought never to be so set. Together with the Preface and the special prefaces it occupies a place of particular solemnity in the Office. The ancient plain-song melodies, and those alone, should be employed here, with the choice either of the Sarum or the Roman Use – in England preferably the former (both these uses have in modern times been well adapted to the English words). Nor should they be accompanied with harmonies on the organ. The 'Comfortable Words', which are peculiar to the English liturgy, should be intoned on one note by the priest without inflexions.

In the early days of the Reformation, even before 1549, the Holy Communion was being celebrated in English, with music for the complete Office on the lines of the Latin Mass. The 'Wanley' part-books in the Bodleian Library (see p. 36) contain as many as ten settings of the entire Mass in English, including *Kyrie, Gloria in excelsis, Credo, Sanctus, Benedictus* and *Agnus Dei*. In one or two of these settings some of the Offertory sentences and post-Communions are included. Two of these ten settings are adaptations of Latin Masses by Taverner, and one is by Heath. Their existence at an even earlier date than that of the First Prayer Book is a matter of great historical interest for liturgiologists as well as for musicians.

During the three years that followed, the full Mass would certainly have been sung in English in the cathedrals. It is almost equally certain that when the English rites were re-sumed after the Marian reaction the custom had changed. Evidence for this is clearly provided by the compositions of the time. The explanation is to be found in the strong counter-reaction that followed the reign of Mary.

Although a large number of English settings of the *Kyrie* and *Credo* were composed in Elizabeth I's reign, there are hardly any of *Gloria in excelsis, Benedictus* or *Agnus Dei*, nor of the *Sanctus*, although after the beginning of the seventeenth century it was a common practice to add that to the *Kyrie* and *Credo*. It has been suggested that composers of those days did set the full Mass, but that only the *Kyrie* and *Credo* were selected for purposes of printing, or for inclusion in the manuscript part-books used by the singers. A wide research among the early part-books, however, makes it clear that there were extremely few exceptions to the custom of ending with the *Credo*. The full settings by Heath and Caustun (two) are pre-Elizabethan; they belong to the Edwardian era, and so, almost certainly, does Tallis's 'Dorian' Service. It is noteworthy that Heath's *Benedictus* and *Agnus Dei*, which are found with the rest of his Communion Service in the Wanley part-books, were omitted by John Day in his *Certaine Notes* (see p. 40) published in 1560. They would therefore seem already to have fallen into disuse, and few English settings of them for liturgical use are known after that date until the middle of the nineteenth century.[1]

Tallis's five-part Service, which is probably an early Elizabethan work, and the compositions of Hooper and Amner which belong to the later Elizabethan period, are exceptional in including *Sanctus* and *Gloria in excelsis*. But both the Short and the Great Services by Byrd, those by Richard Farrant and Morley, and, in Jacobean times, those by Gibbons, Weelkes, Tomkins and a number of other less notable composers of that date, stopped short with *Kyrie* and *Credo*.

Before the close of the sixteenth century the general form of Sunday morning service had come into use which prevailed with little alteration till the latter part of the nineteenth century. This consisted of Mattins and the so-called ante-Communion Service. All this was sung with full music by the choirs, and it ended with the Prayer for the Church militant, followed by the Blessing or 'The grace of our Lord'. There is, however, evidence of a full choral Mass being sung in the time of Charles I at certain cathedrals. Durham is one of these, and so is Exeter and possibly also Worcester. This would be accounted for under the Laudian revival, while Cosin's influence as a prebendary points in this direction at Durham. It was at this same period in all probability that Matthew Jeffreys of Wells, Batten of St Paul's and Child of Windsor each included a single

---

[1] The Service by Nathaniel Pattrick, Organist of Worcester Cathedral (1590–5), printed in full in a modern edition, is no exception. The missing numbers have been adapted.

setting of *Gloria in excelsis* as well as the customary *Sanctus* in their services, though no settings of *Agnus Dei* or *Benedictus qui venit* are known at this period. George Loosemore, organist of Trinity College, Cambridge (1660), also set *Gloria in excelsis*[1] although the other parts of the Service, if indeed he wrote them, are not known to exist: Tudway describes the piece as a 'hymn'.

In the opening years of the eighteenth century it is surprising to find as many as five settings of *Sanctus* and *Gloria in excelsis*. Two of these are by Blow, and one each by Henry Aldrich, Jeremiah Clarke and William Croft; there may have been others. There is also a setting of *Sanctus* and *Gloria in excelsis*[2] of an elaborate character, attributed doubtfully to Croft but certainly belonging to that period. It is for five voices; the *Gloria* is in three movements of some length. This provision of music for the choral celebration of the Holy Communion coincides with the rise of the High Church party in the early years of Queen Anne, when 'Services with choral accompaniments were preferred to sermons' and 'in all the Cathedrals there were weekly celebrations of Holy Communion'.[3] It is recorded[4] that in the Chapel Royal 'the Organ and Voices assisted at *Holy*, *Holy*, *&c.*, and at *Gloria in excelsis*' at the celebration of the Holy Communion.

More singular is the setting of *Gloria in excelsis* and *Sanctus* by Thomas Ebdon (organist of Durham Cathedral, 1763–1811) in his Service in C major. His music happens to be of very slight merit, but its importance lies in the fact that nothing else of the kind is known within a very long period both before and after this date. Evidence that it was composed for practical use is provided by two separate minutes of the Durham Chapter, both of which were entered during Ebdon's tenure of the organistship. On 9 February 1765, 'Ordered that the singing men and choristers attend at the Sacrament on the first Sunday in every month unless such Sunday immediately either precedes or follows one of the Great Festivals, viz.: Christmas, Easter, or Whitsuntide, on which said Festivals their attendance is

[1] Tenbury MS. 795; British Museum, Harl. 7339.
[2] Tenbury MS. 686.
[3] Bishop George Bull, *Defence of the Clergy of England*, p. 45.
[4] Diary of Bishop Nicolson of Carlisle, 4 November 1705.

expected.' A similar minute is dated 20 July 1796. Ebdon's service cannot have been the only one in use.

There is good ground for believing that the customs and
ceremonies that had been re-established by Cosin at Durham
Cathedral in the time of Charles I were revived again in the
reign of Queen Anne and that they continued to be observed
there until a much later date than is generally known. Thus
it is recorded in 1737 that 'no copes are worn at present in any
Cathedral or Collegiate Church in the Ministration of the Holy
Communion except in the Churches of Westminster and Durham'.[1] Another writer states[2] that 'in the Cathedral of Durham
the use of copes was retained until a very late period. In 1628
the virulent Peter Smart attacked Cosin for using them in that
Church. They were not thrown aside until 1760.' That brings
us down to Ebdon's time. The mention of the use of copes at
Westminster recalls the fact that at Purcell's funeral in the
Abbey the whole Chapter assisted 'with their vestments'.[3]

Since the Oxford Movement a very large repertory has
grown up, providing music for the full rendering of the English
'Supper of the Lorde and the Holy Communion, commonly
called the Masse',[4] a term that is no longer associated with
those misunderstandings and controversies which so long cen-
tred round it. This repertory has been built up by musicians
representing various shades of opinion concerning Church ceremony; most of them in more recent times have included settings
of *Benedictus* and *Agnus Dei*, together with *Sanctus* and *Gloria in
excelsis*. It is only since the middle of the nineteenth century that
the entire Office of the Holy Communion has been revived with
suitable musical dignity in accordance with the true tradition
of the English Church. It was many years later still before the
custom of holding such a service weekly on Sundays became
general in cathedrals throughout the country. One of the
earliest occasions is recorded in a letter from Benjamin Webb to

---

[1] *The Rubrick of the Church of England examin'd and consider'd* (London, 1737).
Printed for T. Astley.

[2] *The Fabric Rolls of York Minster*, ed. James Raine (1859), p. 307.

[3] J. A. Westrup, 'Fact and Fiction about Purcell,' *Proceedings of the Musical
Association*, lxii (1935–6), p. 111.

[4] Rubric in the Prayer Book of 1549.

his friend J. M. Neale, the hymnologist, dated 31 December 1847.[1] He wrote: 'At Margaret Chapel[2] they have now got up a complete musical Mass: the Commandments, Epistle, Gospel, Preface, &c., all sung to the ancient music. I venture to assert that there has been nothing so solemn since the Reformation.'

It is sometimes asked to what extent the Communion Service would have been rendered chorally from the Elizabethan period onward on the occasion of ordinations or the consecration of a bishop. Judging from the scanty evidence available, it would seem that the choir usually ceased to function after the Nicene Creed had been sung, and perhaps also a setting of one or two of the Offertory sentences. It is probable that they left the choir-stalls after the Prayer for the Church militant. At coronations in Westminster Abbey the entire service was rendered chorally.

An interesting record of seventeenth-century practice has been preserved by James Clifford, Minor Canon of St Paul's Cathedral, in his *Divine Services and Anthems*, published in 1663; this shows the exact procedure usually followed at the Sunday services not only in his own time but also in the years immediately before the Civil War. Clifford's purpose was to place on record the conditions, as he remembered them, before the churches had been closed, since he feared that many important details might otherwise have become forgotten and neglected. His 'brief directions' are as follows:

The first Service in the morning
After the Psalms a Voluntary on the organ alone. After the first lesson is sung *Te Deum laudamus*. . . . After the second lesson *Benedictus* . . . or *Jubilate*. After the third Collect is sung the first Anthem. After that the Litany. After the Blessing (The Grace of our Lord, &c.) a Voluntary alone on the Organ.

The second or Communion Service
After every Commandment the Prayer, Lord, have mercy upon us. After the Epistle this Ejaculation, Glory be to thee, O Lord. After the Holy Gospel the Nicene Creed. After the Sermon the last Anthem.

---

[1] *Letters of J. M. Neale* (1910), p. 107.
[2] Later known as All Saints', Margaret Street, London, W.1.

At Evening Service

After the Psalms a Voluntary alone by the Organ. After the first lesson *Magnificat*. After the second lesson *Nunc dimittis* or *Deus misereatur*.

William Bird   William Mundy   Mr Strogers   O. Gibbons   Dr Gyles
Dr Child   Thomas Tallis   Elway Bevan   Tho. Tomkins   A. Batten
Mr Portman   Ch. Gibbons

After the third Collect is sung the first Anthem. After the Sermon is sung the last Anthem. ·

The list of twelve musicians refers to the available full settings of the canticles, which, according to Clifford, had been in use at the Chapel Royal and St Paul's Cathedral in the reign of Charles I.

At this date it was customary to sing musical settings of the *Sanctus* as an *Introit* before the 'ante-Communion' Service. Almost all composers after the Restoration included it with *Kyrie* and *Credo*. The insertion of an organ voluntary after the psalms both at the Morning and Evening Service was a custom that prevailed until the latter part of the nineteenth century. For a long time a definite composition was played, but latterly it became usual for the organist to extemporize. Samuel Sebastian Wesley, when organist at Winchester Cathedral (1849–65), was famous for his extempore playing after the psalms, before the anthem, and at the end of the service. The long extempore performance on the organ before the anthem on Sunday afternoons was a popular feature at all the English cathedrals.

This ordering of the church service, as recorded by Clifford, is what Samuel Pepys was accustomed to when he attended the Chapel Royal on a Sunday morning in the early days of the Restoration, except that there only one anthem was sung, after the sermon. His comments on it were usually coupled with some observation about the sermon. Thus, on 7 October 1660, when Dr Spurstow, Master of St Catherine's, Cambridge, was the preacher, Pepys remarks: 'A poor dry sermon; but a very good anthem of Captn. Cooke's afterwards.' Conversely, on the following Sunday the preacher had his approval and the singers were at fault: 'An anthem, ill sung, which made the King laugh.' On 8 January 1665 Pepys noted: 'A good sermon, and afterwards a brave anthem upon the 150 Psalm, where upon the word "trumpet" very good musique was made.' The sermon on that occasion was preached by Dr Beaumont, Master of Peterhouse, Cambridge.

CHAPTER 4

The Edwardian Period

It is fortunate that enough of the church music of Edward VI's reign (1547–53) and the few years immediately preceding it is available today to make possible a general survey. A few manuscripts have survived the ruthless destruction wrought upon such documents at various periods of English history by religious fanatics, and even by order of Parliament. Furthermore, John Day printed and published a collection of services and anthems in 1560 (see p. 40). It is regrettable that the Wanley part-books (see p. 36)[1] dating from *c.* 1546–7, which provide the largest amount of available information, are imperfect. It is also unfortunate that no composer's name is recorded in the manuscript. There is another valuable manuscript belonging to the same period in the British Museum.[2] It is a small collection, but contains the only known text of Tallis's *Benedictus* for men's voices in four parts. There are also settings of the canticles, including two of *Te Deum*, two of *Nunc dimittis*, and also a setting of the response to the Commandments, though this had no place in the Prayer Book before 1552: 'Lord have merchi upon us and encline our harts to kipe this lawe.'

Not a little of the music found in later sixteenth-century manuscripts must also have been written in pre-Elizabethan, and therefore, in all probability, pre-Marian days. But except in the case of composers who are known to have died before the accession of Elizabeth I (1558), no absolute certainty as regards these can be established. Internal evidence of style can be very deceptive for determining dates within such narrow limits. But

---

[1] Bodleian Library, Mus. Sch. e. 420–2.
[2] Royal App. 74–6.

in the case of the music printed by Day, and that found in the earlier manuscripts, there is no uncertainty about the date.

It was a basic principle of the Reformation that the services were to be something 'understanded of the people'. Cranmer's reference to fitting to every syllable a note (see p. 24) was in accordance with this principle. A precise ruling in this matter is to be found in the Royal Injunctions delivered to the Dean and Chapter of Lincoln Minster on 14 April 1548.[1] It was ordered (§ 25) that

> they shall fromhensforthe synge or say no Anthemes [i.e. anti-phons] off our lady or other saynts but onely of our lorde And them not in laten but choseyng owte the best and moste soundyng to[2] cristen religion they shall turne the same into Englishe settyng therunto a playn and distincte note, for every sillable one, they shall singe them and none other.

The reference here is to the so-called 'votive antiphons', mostly in honour of the Virgin Mary (e.g. *Salve regina*), which in the pre-Reformation Church were sung before the altar after Com-pline, and often at other times as well. It is quite possible that the injunction is primarily concerned with English adaptations of plainsong and is therefore similar to Cranmer's recommen-dation for the setting of his processions. However, polyphonic settings of the texts of votive antiphons had been in use in England for at least two centuries before this, and it may well be that the authors of the injunction had these in mind as well, though clearly the principle of one note to a syllable is less easy to apply in polyphony, particularly at cadences. It was in any case inevitable, if the insistence on clear enunciation of the English words was to be obeyed, that composers should exert themselves to write the simplest possible polyphony. That they did so is borne out by the examples of English church music that survive from the early years of the Reformation.

A good deal was lost by this change of style. It meant the end of those long melismas which are one of the glories of pre-Reformation church music – for example, in the work of

---

[1] *Statutes of Lincoln*, iii, p. 592.
[2] i.e. related to, tending towards.

Fayrfax,[1] the composers of the Eton Choirbook[2] and Taverner.[3] It does not follow, however, that musicians were unsympathetic towards the principle of clear enunciation, or that their artistic instincts were cramped by clerical authority. Tallis, Tye and others were left free to continue, and did continue, to write Latin motets and other music for the older rites, and ample scope remained in that direction for the unrestrained expression of their genius.

The Wanley manuscript, as already mentioned, includes ten settings of the full Communion Service in English, including *Gloria in excelsis*, *Sanctus*, *Benedictus* and *Agnus Dei*. There are also five settings of *Magnificat* and *Nunc dimittis*, one of which is by William Whytbroke, three settings of *Te Deum* and *Benedictus*, three settings of the *Lord's Prayer* and two of the Litany, besides a large number of anthems. The litanies are early examples of the harmonization of the melodies issued with Cranmer's version in 1544. The first of these (No. 69) is beautiful in its simplicity (the melody, in the tenor, is supplied from Cranmer's book):

The other setting (No. 49) is less satisfying; but it is suitable for men's voices when the boys are absent:

---

[1] *Corpus Mensurabilis Musicae*, 17, ed. E. B. Warren, 3 vols., American Institute of Musicology.

[2] *Musica Britannica*, x–xii, ed. F. Ll. Harrison.

[3] *Tudor Church Music*, i and iii.

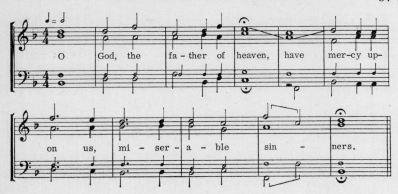

The bass part of another harmonized Litany is to be found in a manuscript[1] dating certainly before 1549. It fits exactly with Cranmer's melodies. It is therefore quite simple to reconstruct the other two parts.[2]

Some of the compositions in the Wanley manuscript are probably earlier than anything written for the English rites by Tallis or Sheppard, or by any of the other composers who have been identified in this anonymous collection. Tallis was living undisturbed at Waltham Abbey until 1540, whereas some of the versions of the words of the canticles in this manuscript are English translations from Marshall's Primer of 1535. Other versions found here are from Hilsey's Primer of 1539, and others again from Henry VIII's of 1545.

The strictness with which the principle of simplicity was observed may be illustrated by quoting examples. The following (No. 58) is the beginning of *Gloria in excelsis* in an anonymous Mass:[3]

[1] British Museum, Add. 34,191.
[2] *Four settings of the Litany from early sources*, ed. E. H. Fellowes & S. H. Nicholson (The Faith Press).
[3] The bar-lines and the tenor part are editorial.

D

The next example gives the opening of one of the settings of *Magnificat* (No. 3):[1]

[1] The tenor part is editorial.

Tallis's 'Dorian' Service is hardly more ambitious.

That beautiful effects could be produced by these simple methods is illustrated by a setting of one of the post-Communion sentences (No. 82):

Another anonymous and attractive piece in this manuscript is *O Lord the Maker of all thing*[1] (No. 48), set in the simplest manner, line by line, and 'for every note a syllable'. The words are from Henry VIII's Primer of 1545.

In a few instances the composers have been identified from other sources. Among them are *Praise we the Father* and *Praise the Lord* by Robert Okeland; *O Eternal God* by Robert Johnson (d. *c.* 1560); *Let all the congregation* by Thomas Caustun (d. 1569); *I give you a new commandment* and *Submit yourselves* by John Sheppard; *If ye love me*, *This is my commandment* and *Hear the voice* by Tallis; *Magnificat* and *Nunc dimittis* by Whytbroke. Mention has already been made (p. 27) of Heath's full Communion Service, and the adaptations to English words of two of John Taverner's Masses (Nos. 86 and 87). No. 86 is adapted from *The Meane*[2] *Mass* (also known as *Missa sine nomine*),[3] and No. 87

---

[1] Not to be confused with the later setting of these words by William Mundy (see p. 60).

[2] The 'mean' (Latin *medius*) was properly a voice-part intermediate between the treble (*triplex*) and the *contratenor* or tenor. Where there is no treble part it was the highest part in a composition and frequently indicates a part written for the normal range of a boy's voice.

[3] *Tudor Church Music*, i, p. 50.

from the Mass entitled in the Peterhouse part-books *In Small Devotion*.[1] These English adaptations seem to have been made by an unskilled hand. They serve to show, as they must have done at the time, that no real satisfaction could be derived from such methods, but that the need of music for the English rites in the English language could adequately be met only with original work. The section of the *Credo* 'I believe in the Holy Ghost', which is omitted in the original Latin setting of both these Masses, was supplied by the arranger from other material in the original text, which in its turn was omitted in the English version.

John Day's publication of 1560 carries the strong presumption that all the music included in it was pre-Elizabethan and therefore in all probability pre-Marian. The full title is: *Certaine notes set forthe in foure and three partes, to be sung at the Mornyng Communion and Evenyng Praier, very necessairie for the Church of Christe to be frequented and used: and unto them added divers Godly praiers and Psalms in the like forme to the honor and prayse of God. Imprinted at London over Aldersgate beneath S. Martins by John Day. 1560. Cum gratia et privilegio Regiae Maiestatis.* A second edition was published in 1565 under a rather different title: *Mornyng and Evenyng Praier and Communion, set forthe in foure partes to be song in churches, both for men and children wyth dyvers other godly praiers and Anthems of sundry men's doynges.*

This is the earliest printed collection of English church music. It contains twenty anthems, of which at least eight are found also in the Wanley manuscript; two full services by THOMAS CAUSTUN which include *Venite, Sanctus* and *Gloria in excelsis*. Caustun is also represented by a third *Magnificat* and *Nunc dimittis* and six anthems; it would seem that he enjoyed greater popularity at that period than any one else. Yet no one today would think of comparing his work with that of Tallis and Tye, or others among his contemporaries. He was a member of the Chapel Royal and died in 1569. Nothing else is known of his

---

[1] *Tudor Church Music*, i, p. 70. Dr F. Ll. Harrison (*Music & Letters*, xlvi [1965], p. 382) suggests that the title is a copyist's misreading of 'S. W(ilhelmi) devotio', on the ground that in this Mass the composer uses material from his antiphon 'Christe Jesu, pastor bone' (*Tudor Church Music*, iii, p. 73), the original words of which were probably 'O Wilhelme, pastor bone', an antiphon of St William of York.

personal history. As a composer he gives the impression of
being a man of sincere religious feeling but no more than an
enthusiastic amateur. Judged by the standards of his contemporaries his technical skill was only moderate, if Day's text
is to be trusted. Yet the sincerity of his style enables him to
hold a place in the cathedral lists of the twentieth century in
spite of technical defects. Caustun was fond of phrases in which
two parts could run together in tenths or sixths. The following
characteristic phrase occurs three times in slightly different
form in the *Benedictus* of one of his services[1]:

*F in the original

and again, but more awkwardly, in *Magnificat* (notice the consecutive fifths):

O sacred and holy banquet, which sometimes appears in cathedral
lists and is ascribed to Caustun, is a modern adaptation of
selected passages from one of his settings of *Venite.*

[1] *Tudor Church Music,* 8vo ed., Nos. 94 and 95.

Three names stand out conspicuously in this period: Christopher Tye, Thomas Tallis and John Marbeck. John Sheppard and Robert Johnson may also be added to this group, although probably not much of their work for the English rites was produced so early as this; in any case the fame of these two composers rests much more upon their music for the Latin rites of the Church. The available material for discussing what was actually the earliest stage in the history of English cathedral music is virtually limited to the work of these five composers, together with that of those unnamed composers whose music fills so many pages of the Wanley manuscript.

Since CHRISTOPHER TYE (c. 1500–73) was the eldest, his work may be taken first. It would be a mistake to suppose that Day's selection adequately represents the whole repertory at that time, small though that repertory must still have been. Nevertheless it is strange that no work of Tye has a place in his publication. Most of Tye's English church music must belong to the pre-Elizabethan period, and its simple character and style are in keeping with this opinion. It fits in, too, with his tenure of office at Ely Cathedral. He was appointed master of the choristers at Ely in 1541, after having served in the choir of King's College, Cambridge, where he began his career as a chorister. He was also simultaneously a member of the Chapel Royal during the reign of Edward VI.[1] He continued in office at Ely throughout the reign of Mary and saw many changes in the form of church service during the twenty years he spent at the cathedral before his resignation in 1561. By that time he had been ordained. He subsequently held several benefices, and died as rector of Doddington, in the Isle of Ely.

Of the fourteen English anthems by this composer that survive complete, *I will exalt thee*, with its second section *Sing unto the Lord*,[2] is the most familiar. Several of Tye's anthems are of much greater length than those of Tallis and others of his contemporaries. *I have loved* is a setting of Psalm cxvi. 1–8 (*Dilexi quoniam*), which is more familiar in the Prayer Book version: 'I am well pleased that the Lord hath heard the voice

[1] Title-page of his *Actes of the Apostles* (1553), for which see p. 44.
[2] *Tudor Church Music*, 8vo ed., No. 59.

of my prayer.' This is the first psalm for Vespers of the Dead in the Roman rite, and it suggests that Tye and other early composers tended towards a choice of words with which they were already familiar in Latin. It may well be that in this particular instance Tye had in mind a funeral anthem based on the Latin text. *From the depth* and *Deliver us* look like early experiments; but *I lift my heart to thee*[1] and *I will exalt thee*,[2] are fine examples of the Tudor style of anthem, particularly the jubilant opening of the second part of the latter, which shows that simplicity did not preclude imitation:

The Evening Service in G minor, often attributed to Tye, is almost certainly the work of Osbert Parsley,[3] his contemporary at the neighbouring cathedral of Norwich (see p. 56). On the other hand a *Nunc dimittis* in F major is undoubtedly Tye's composition.[4] Both the style of the music and the version of the words point to an early date and this is confirmed by the fact

---

[1] An adaptation to English words of the instrumental piece *Amavit* (British Museum, Add. 31,390, fo. 112).

[2] *Tudor Church Music*, 8vo ed., No. 59.

[3] *Ibid.*, No. 87.

[4] British Museum, Add. 30,480-3.

that it occurs anonymously in the Wanley manuscript (No. 7).
It opens thus:

The words continue: 'According to thy promise, for mine eyes
have seen the Saviour sent from thee.' The *Gloria* ends with
'Always so be it' in place of 'Amen'.

In more recent times a number of adaptations have been
made of 'chapters' from Tye's setting of *The Actes of the Apostles*,
published in 1553 with a dedication to Edward VI.[1] The very
pedestrian metrical version of the words, as well as the music,
was his own composition. The best known of these adaptations
is that sung to *Laudate nomen Domini*, with the English alternative
O come, ye servants of the Lord: The original words were:

> The iiij Chapter
> When that the people taught they had
> There came to them doutles
> Priests and rulers as men nye mad
> And Eke the Saduces,
> Whome it greved that they should move
> The people and them leade
> That Jesus Christe by powre above
> Should ryse up from the deade.

---

[1] Modern edition in M. Frost, *English & Scottish Psalm & Hymn Tunes c. 1543–
1677* (1953), pp. 343–73.

THOMAS TALLIS (d. 1585), like Tye, produced his most distinguished work for the Latin rite. The date of his birth is unknown, but it may be placed at least as early as 1505, since he was described as 'verie aged' in 1577,[1] an expression that must have meant at least over 70. Also he appears to have been in a leading position at Waltham Abbey before its dissolution in 1540. In earlier years he had held appointments at Dover Priory (in 1532) and St Mary-at-Hill, London (in 1537). After leaving Waltham he was for a short period a lay-clerk at Canterbury, and from c. 1543 a member of the Chapel Royal. He was buried in the chancel of St Alphege Church, Green-wich, where he lived in his later years. The full text of the rhymed inscription engraved upon his tomb is reproduced on a mural tablet in the church. The original tombstone was destroyed when the church was rebult in the eighteenth century.

A comparison of Tallis's Litany with the settings found in the Wanley manuscript suggests that it is early Elizabethan.[2] The 'Dorian' Service may with fair certainty be assigned to the Edwardian period. Much of it is constructed on a very simple principle not unlike that of a chant, with repeated phrases beginning with three minims and following each other in sequential treatment, e.g. at the opening of the *Te Deum*:

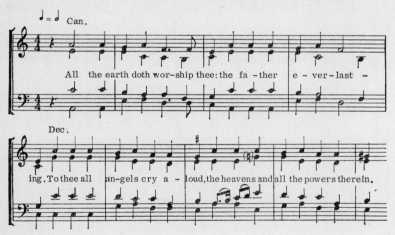

---

[1] Hatfield House MSS., C.P., 160, 134.
[2] For a discussion see p. 54.

Similarly in the *Credo*:

And was cruci fied al - so for us un - der Pontius Pi - - late.

The whole of this melodic material is exactly repeated for the words beginning 'And ascended into heaven' down to 'shall have no end'. *Venite*, in accordance with the practice of the time, is set in full like the other canticles.[1] This service also includes *Sanctus* and *Gloria in excelsis*, as does a five-part service of which the bass part alone survives.[2]

Tallis's *Benedictus* for four men's voices undoubtedly belongs to the Edwardian period, since it is found in a manuscript of that date.[3] Yet it seems far more mature than the 'Dorian' Service. The verbal text of the second verse is: 'And hath lifted up an horn of salvation for us.' The setting begins:

Bless - ed be the Lord God of Is - ra - el:

for he hath vi-si-ted and redeem - -ed his peo - - - ple.

---

[1] This setting was omitted by Boyce (*Cathedral Music*, i, p. 2), who substituted a chant.

[2] St John's College, Oxford, MS. 181.

[3] British Museum, Royal App. 75–6.

Seventeen English anthems by Tallis are known. Besides the three in the Wanley manuscript two more were included by Day: *O Lord, in thee is all my trust* and *Remember not, O Lord*; but he omitted *This is my commandment*. *O Lord, give thy Holy Spirit* seems with great probability to belong to the Elizabethan period, and it will accordingly be referred to in the following chapter (see p. 52). The other eleven cannot be dated with any certainty, but they are constructed on the same simple design and may all belong to this early period. *Remember not, Lord* is by contrast more extended in form. *I give you a new commandment*, attributed to Tallis in the keyboard arrangement in the Mulliner book,[1] is by Sheppard (see p. 57). *I call and cry*[2] is a sixteenth-century adaptation to English words of *O sacrum convivium*.[3] Altogether eight such adaptations are known,[4] four of them printed by Barnard. *All people that on earth do dwell* is an adaptation 'from Tallis' made by Aldrich *c.* 1700,[5] without any indication of its origin. *Come Holy Ghost*, ascribed to Tallis by Aldrich, is of doubtful authenticity. In choosing texts for his anthems Tallis was evidently impressed with the beauty of chapters 13–15 of St John's Gospel. He also took verses from the Psalms.

JOHN MARBECK was born probably about 1510, for his son Roger, afterwards Provost of Oriel College, Oxford, was born in 1536.[6] His only surviving compositions[7] are a Mass, *Per arma justitiae*, two antiphons – *Domine Jesu Christe* and *Ave Dei patris filia* – and a carol to English words (*A virgine and mother*), all probably written before he was arrested in 1544 (see p. 49). His *Booke of Common praier noted* was published in 1550. The 'noting' of the portion used 'at the Communion' is now so widely known that it is sometimes forgotten that he also 'noted' the Order of Mattins and Evensong, the Office for the Burial of the Dead, and 'the Communion when there is a burial'.

[1] British Museum, Add. 30,513, fo. 51.
[2] *Tudor Church Music*, 8vo. ed., No. 74.
[3] *Tudor Church Music*, vi, p. 210.
[4] See the list in Grove's *Dictionary of Music*, 5th ed. (1954), p. 299.
[5] Christ Church, Oxford, MSS. 1220–4.
[6] E. H. Fellowes, *Organists and Masters of the Choristers of St. George's Chapel in Windsor Castle* (1939), p. 12.
[7] *Tudor Church Music*, x, pp. 165 ff.

There is virtually no genuine plainsong in Marbeck's book. What he did was to adapt the music of the Latin rite to English words and to add original melodies of his own. The 'noting' of the Versicles and Responses forms the foundation on which almost all the subsequent harmonized settings are constructed. The setting of *Te Deum* is an adaptation of the Ambrosian melody. *Benedictus* is set to tone 5 and tone 8, 1st ending. For Evensong Marbeck chose tones 1, 4th ending and 8, 1st ending for *Magnificat*, and tones 5 and 7, 4th ending for *Nunc dimittis*. In the Communion Service *Gloria in excelsis* and *Credo* are original compositions, but *Sanctus* and *Benedictus* are derived from a mode 2 plainsong setting,[1] though very much compressed, and *Agnus Dei* appears also to be distantly related to a Sarum melody.[2] The Offertories and post-Communions are original compositions.[3]

Marbeck lived for 35 years after this book was published, carrying on his work as one of the organists at St George's Chapel; and it is strange that, as far as can be discovered, he should have composed no more music. It must have been a severe disappointment to him that the *Booke of Common praier noted* so soon fell into neglect, but it must also have become apparent to him, as he superintended the daily choral services at Windsor, that the taste for unison singing had been entirely superseded.

If Marbeck were alive today he would probably say that he was a theologian rather than a musician. He was the author of several books, most of which involved much biblical knowledge and research. His Concordance of the Bible, also published in 1550, was a work of immense labour. He himself described it as a 'houge volume'; even in its final reduced form it contains over 900 folios, each divided into three columns. In this work Marbeck proved himself, when still a comparatively young man, to be a theological student, a Latin scholar and a person of exceptional courage and perseverance. It is the earliest concordance of the whole of the English Bible ever made.

---

[1] *Graduale Sarisburiense*, ed. W. H. Frere (1894–5), pl. 15* (Vatican No. XI).
[2] *Ibid.*, pl. 18*.
[3] For a detailed account see R. R. Terry, 'John Merbecke', *Proceedings of the Musical Association*, xlv (1918–19), pp. 75–96.

Every word is accompanied by its Latin equivalent; and the difficulties which he met and overcame in the course of its production are astounding. In March 1544 he, with two of his colleagues in the Windsor choir, was arrested and in his own words[1] 'quickly condempned and Judged to death, for the copiyng out of a worke, made by the greate Clerke Master Jhon Calvin, written against thesame sixe articles . . .: thesame tyme was my greate work, emong other, taken from me and utterly lost'. This work was his Concordance. After his release and pardon Marbeck settled down again at Windsor, and with amazing courage 'began againe therewith and writt out thesame'. He experienced a bitter disappointment when, after this enormous double labour, no publisher could be persuaded to print it for the reason that a book of this size would have to be priced at a figure which no purchaser would consent to pay for it. Undeterred, he 'yet once again a newe writte out the same, in suche sorte as the worke now appereth'. In this reduced form, 'huge' though it still is, it survives today, although copies are extremely rare.

The English work of the Scottish composer ROBERT JOHN-SON (c. 1490–1565) and of JOHN SHEPPARD at this period is so slight as to call for no detailed comment. Sheppard's English services will be mentioned in the following chapter (see p. 57), since they probably belong to the early Elizabethan period.

---

[1] *A Concordance*, preface.

CHAPTER 5

The Early Elizabethan Period

Elizabeth I succeeded her sister in November 1558. In the following April two Acts of Parliament came into force which were of the highest importance. The Act of Supremacy restored to the Crown the jurisdiction over the State Ecclesiastical and all spiritual courts and persons; it also repealed all the Acts made in Queen Mary's reign dealing with religious matters. And the Act of Uniformity enforced the use of the revised Prayer Book, which was to be taken into general use at the Feast of St John the Baptist (24 June) in the same year. Considerable opposition was encountered, especially from the Marian bishops and beneficed clergy, before these measures were passed.

To supplement these Acts of Parliament a large number of Injunctions were issued for the guidance of the Church, particularly in the difficult interval between the deprivation of the Marian ecclesiastics and the establishment of their successors. No. 49 of these Injunctions has special reference to cathedral music. It ordered that whereas in collegiate churches and some parish churches there were endowments 'for the mayntey-naunce of men and children, to vse singing in the church, by meanes wherof, the lawdable science of musicke hath ben had in estimation, & preserued in knowledge', the queen commanded that 'no alteration be made of suche assignements of lyuyng, as heretofore hath ben appoynted to the vse of syngyng or musicke in the Churche, but that the same so remayne'. And 'for the comfortyng of suche that delyght in musicke, it may be permitted that in the begynnyng, or in the ende of common prayers, eyther at mornyng or euenyng, there may be song an Hymne, or such like songue, to the prayse of almighty god, in the best sort of melodie and musicke that maye be conueniently deuised, hauing respect that the sentence of the Hymne may be understanded and perceyued'.[1] The word 'hymn', as employed here in reference to cathedral music, means 'anthem'.

The queen had been brought up in childhood with ideas that were strongly opposed to the Papacy. At her accession to the throne she was especially anxious to recover the position of supremacy held by her father. At the same time she was fond of pomp and ceremony in all matters, and this fact influenced her attitude towards the ritual of the church services. In the Chapel Royal, by her own command no doubt, 'a cross stood upon the Altar and two candlesticks and two tapers burning'.[2] This was in striking contrast to the Puritan spirit prevailing in her brother Edward's reign.

In effect this was the third drastic change in the forms of worship within the course of a single decade. Nor was there any certainty that further changes might not follow in the near future, while the Calvinists and Roman Catholics were struggling for supremacy. The queen was 25 years of age and unmarried; the heir to the throne was therefore her cousin, Mary Queen of Scots, who had just married the Dauphin, who shortly afterwards succeeded to the throne of France as Francis II. If Elizabeth had died early in 1560, or even shortly after the death of the French king, there might have been a further reaction. Church musicians may very well have wondered whether it was worth while to resume the task of supplying music for the English rite. Indeed, very little seems to have been composed in the early years of Elizabeth's reign. It is significant that Day waited nearly two years after Mary's death before venturing to publish his *Certaine Notes* (see p. 40) in 1560. The available repertory of services and anthems cannot have been large at this date, and what did exist must have been almost entirely pre-Elizabethan.

The fact that a second edition of Day's collection appeared in 1565 is evidence that it was widely used; but it may be argued from this that not much new music was making its

---

[1] *Iniunctions geuen by the Queenes Maiestie* (1559).
[2] J. Strype, *Annals of the Reformation*, i, p. 275.

appearance in manuscript to supplement it. It becomes a matter of particular interest to consider who were actively engaged in musical composition at the date of Elizabeth's accession. Tye was at least 55 years old. Tallis and Osbert Parsley were about 50, and Sheppard was probably not much younger than these. Robert Johnson was an elderly man and died very shortly after this date. William Mundy may have been under 30. Robert White, Robert Parsons and Richard and John Farrant were certainly under 30. Byrd was only 15, and Morley an infant. William Mundy, White, Parsons and the two Farrants were the only new composers of note to appear in the field of church music at this period. The four older men were still in full activity, and as they all excelled chiefly in their work for the Latin rite, it may be supposed that they were far from idle during the Marian period. Tallis is known to have been in favour with Mary, who in 1557 granted him a lease of the manor of Minster in the Isle of Thanet. That Tye continued to write some music at this period is shown by the fact that his Latin motet *In quo corriget* is dated 1568;[1] but it is probable that most, if not all, of his English anthems were written while he was organist of Ely.

Although it is impossible to assign even approximate dates to the music of these composers on internal evidence alone, yet in the case of Tallis it may not be unreasonable to offer a tentative opinion with regard to the compositions which may belong to the first fifteen years or so of Elizabeth's reign. It will be remembered that in 1577, when he and William Byrd petitioned the queen for a lease to be granted to them, Tallis was described as 'now verie aged'.[2] It may be presumed he had given up composing before that; but as he was actively associated with Byrd in the production of the *Cantiones sacrae* published in 1575, there can be no doubt about his continued activities until shortly before that date. Reasons have already been given for thinking that most if not all of his English anthems are early works, together with the 'Dorian' Service and the four-part *Benedictus*. By exception *O Lord, give thy Holy*

[1] Bodleian Library, Mus. Sch. e. 423.
[2] Hatfield House MSS., C.P. 160, 134.

Spirit[1] must almost certainly belong to Tallis's later years. In a general way it is riper in character and it has some resemblance to Loosemore's *O Lord, increase our faith*. But the most noteworthy feature is the use of the interval of the augmented fifth, a very early example of what became more general at the close of the century. A characteristic clash between F♮ and F♯ will also be observed, but that was a common usage throughout the century:

It may be that the *Preces and Responses*, the Litany, the five-part full Service, and the five-part *Te Deum* belong to the early Elizabethan period. Tallis's hymn-tunes are actually dated 1567, and the psalm settings are, with scarcely any doubt, Elizabethan. There are two independent, if somewhat similar, versions of the *Preces and Responses*. The five-part version, printed in Barnard's *Selected Church Musick* in 1641 is certainly authentic. The four-part version, printed anonymously by Edward Lowe in 1661, appears to be an adaptation.[2]

Settings of the *Preces and Responses* in an elaborate manner,

---

[1] *Tudor Church Music*, 8vo ed., No. 68.
[2] See *Six settings of the Preces and Responses by Tudor Composers*, ed. I. Atkins & E. H. Fellowes.

E

using Marbeck's melodies for the tenor voice, were much in
vogue in the latter part of the sixteenth century. Similar settings
of a festal character were composed by Morley and Byrd, and
at a rather later date by Tomkins. It is unlikely that Tallis
anticipated this vogue earlier than the Elizabethan period. For
the same reason his Litany may be similarly dated. Whether
he wrote this for four or five voices has been the subject of
controversy. It was the opinion of the editors of *Tudor Church
Music*[1] that the five-part version alone is genuine and that the
four-part version was an adaptation of this. Tallis's setting
ended with the Lesser Litany. The music to the part following
the *Lord's Prayer* that has been usually printed with Tallis's
Litany is an adaptation from his *Responses* made by Aldrich late
in the seventeenth century. Another version to complete the
Litany has been adapted in the present century from the
material which Tallis wrote for the first part.[2]

Tallis composed three groups of psalm settings. The second
deals with Psalms 110 and 132, which are two of the proper
psalms for Christmas Day at Evensong. The long Psalm 89 is
omitted. The other two groups consist of the first four and the
last four sections of Psalm 119, the regular psalms for the 24th
and 26th evenings of the month. Evidently Tallis designed the
three groups as a complete scheme for the three consecutive
evenings – Christmas Eve, Christmas Day and the following
evening. Since no Proper Psalms for the great festivals were
tabulated in the 1549 Prayer Book (they appeared first at the
end of 1552), it is clear that Tallis's Christmas scheme dates
from Elizabeth's reign.

Fortune seems to have dealt particularly harshly with Tallis's
English work, in that of his services only the 'Dorian' has
survived complete. This has resulted in a false estimate of his
music for the English rite. In comparison with his Latin motets
his anthems are of small consequence; and to say that is not
to disparage the rare beauty of *If ye love me*.[3] But the fragments
that survive of his full service for five parts and his five-part

[1] *Tudor Church Music*, vi, p. xix.
[2] *Four settings of the Litany from early sources*, ed. E. H. Fellowes & S. H. Nicholson.
[3] *Tudor Church Music*, 8vo ed., No. 69.

Te Deum,[1] which probably belonged to another complete service, suggest strongly that they were compositions that would compare favourably with the services of any of the Elizabethans, not even excepting Byrd. They show that he was by no means out of sympathy with the style of music required for the English Church. The full service is described in the manuscript as 'of five parts two in one'. Only the bass part is known to exist.[2] It includes *Venite, Te Deum, Benedictus, Kyrie, Credo, Sanctus, Gloria in excelsis, Magnificat* and *Nunc dimittis*. Presumably two parts are in canon, but it would appear unlikely that the term 'two in one' carries that meaning throughout the entire service. That it is written in free imitative counter-point is clearly indicated by the bass part, much in the style of the five-part *Te Deum*. The composer did not hesitate to repeat verbal phrases, especially at a point of climax.

The whole Psalter translated into English Metre by Matthew Parker, Archbishop of Canterbury from 1559 to 1575, was printed (but not published) in 1567. It included a series of eight hymn-tunes by Tallis, followed by an additional tune, making nine in all.[3] Tallis designed them to express various moods and sentiments: their 'nature' is described as follows:

1. The first is meeke: devout to see:
2. The second sad: in maiesty.
3. The third doth rage: and roughly brayth.[4]
4. The fourth doth fawne: and flattry playeth,
5. The fyfth deligth: and laugheth the more,
6. The sixt bewayleth: it weepeth full sore,
7. The seventh tredeth stoute: in froward race,
8. The eyghte goeth milde: in modest pace.

The eighth of these is the well-known 'Canon', now associated with Bishop Ken's *Glory to thee, my God, this night,* in the

---

[1] A reconstruction of the *Te Deum* is published in *Tudor Church Music,* 8vo ed., No. 72.

[2] St John's College, Oxford, MS. 181.

[3] Modern edition in M. Frost, *English & Scottish Psalm & Hymn Tunes c. 1543–1677* (1953), pp. 374–93.

[4] This tune (No. 92 in the English Hymnal) was used by Vaughan Williams in his *Fantasia on a theme by Thomas Tallis* (1910, revised 1913 and 1919).

abbreviated version first printed by Ravenscroft in 1621. It is
given here in its original form:

The extra tune, set to *Come Holy Ghost, eternal God,* is that
subsequently known as 'Tallis's Ordinal'. It is familiar in
modern usage in association with the hymn *O Holy Spirit, Lord
of grace.* It is very unlikely that any of Tallis's tunes were sung,
except privately, in his lifetime, since the book was withdrawn
after it had been set up by the printer.

The English work of OSBERT PARSLEY (1511–85) is of small
importance compared with his Latin compositions.[1] He belonged to the same generation as Tallis and Tye. He was for
more than fifty years a lay-clerk of Norwich Cathedral. His
Evening Service in G minor was attributed to Tye in early
eighteenth-century manuscripts,[2] and it was widely accepted as

---

[1] *Tudor Church Music,* x, pp. 237 ff.
[2] Ely Cathedral MSS.; British Museum, Harl. 7337, fo. 72[v].

Tye's in the nineteenth century, when it was first edited and printed by Rimbault. It is almost certainly by Parsley. In the early Peterhouse and Durham manuscripts it is ascribed alternatively to Tye and to Parsley; but the Morning Service is assigned to Parsley alone in all the manuscripts. Since the *Gloria* of *Nunc dimittis* is identical with that of *Benedictus*, and much of the melodic material of the Morning Service is repeated in the Evening Canticles, it is evident that both are the work of one and the same composer. A *Te Deum* and *Benedictus* in F major by Parsley also survive.

JOHN SHEPPARD did not long survive the accession of Elizabeth I, but his services may belong to this period although certain of his anthems are known to have been earlier. His 'First' Service, as it is described in the early manuscripts,[1] is a fine work for men's voices in four parts, written in a free contrapuntal style. He wrote two other Morning and Evening Services and two settings of *Te Deum* and *Magnificat* for English use. Unfortunately these survive only in fragmentary condition. The opening section of his anthem *I give you a new commandment* will give some idea of the simple directness of his music, of which there is also evidence in his settings for the Latin rite:

[1] Royal College of Music, MSS. 1045–51.

Sheppard was a prolific composer. His Latin church music includes six Masses and more than 60 motets. He was appointed master of the choristers at Magdalen College, Oxford, in 1541 and was a member of the Chapel Royal from 1552.

It remains to consider the work of the younger men in the first years of Elizabeth's reign: Robert White, Richard and John Farrant, William Mundy and Robert Parsons.

ROBERT WHITE (*c.* 1530–74) is first heard of in 1560, when he took the Mus. B. degree at Cambridge. In 1562 he succeeded Tye as master of the choristers at Ely Cathedral and married his daughter. From Ely he seems to have gone to Chester Cathedral; and ultimately, about 1570, he became master of the choristers at Westminster Abbey. White's English work is of very small importance in comparison with his Latin compositions.[1] He wrote no English setting of the canticles, and only four English anthems survive complete. Of these *O praise God in his holiness* for eight voices is outstanding.[2] Reasons have been advanced for thinking that it may have been written before Elizabeth's reign. It is true that the version of the words dates from 1548, but that does not necessarily fix the date of the composition. On the evidence of its style it is not unreasonable to assign it to the early years of Elizabeth when he was at Ely.

The church music of RICHARD FARRANT (d. 1581) may safely be dated in the first half of Elizabeth's reign. His output seems surprisingly small when it is remembered that he was engaged upon choir work for the greater part of his life in association with Marbeck at St George's Chapel, Windsor. It is well known that he was much occupied throughout his

---

[1] *Tudor Church Music,* v.

[2] For the arguments concerning the authenticity of this work and of the four-part version see *ibid.,* pp. xxvi–vii.

career with the dramatic activities of the choristers, both at the Chapel Royal and at Windsor, and these may have absorbed his chief interest. He was appointed master of the choristers at St George's Chapel in 1564. His two short anthems *Hide not thou thy face* and *Call to remembrance*[1] are among the most beautiful things of their kind in the entire repertory of English church music. *Lord, for thy tender mercy's sake* is not by Farrant. In the seventeenth century it was attributed to the elder John Hilton but was never ascribed to Farrant before the latter part of the eighteenth century. In the so-called 'Batten' organ book[2] the anthem *When as we sat in Babylon* is attributed to Richard Farrant, but no text of the voice-parts is known. His Service in A minor,[3] like his two anthems, has the distinction of having kept its place continuously in cathedral usage. In the early manuscripts it is variously described as his 'high' or 'short' or 'old' Service. It consists of *Venite, Te Deum, Benedictus, Kyrie, Credo, Magnificat* and *Nunc dimittis*. This is one of the finest of the Elizabethan services; certain harmonic features in it are of an unusual character at that date.

There is evidence that Farrant composed other services. Fragmentary text of a 'Service in F with verses' is among the Durham Cathedral manuscripts. Richard, however, must not be confused with the two, or possibly three, John Farrants of the next generation. The Service in D minor is certainly the work of one of the two John Farrants who were successively organists of Salisbury Cathedral. The elder JOHN FARRANT was appointed a lay-clerk at Salisbury in 1571, having formerly been organist of Ely and Bristol Cathedrals. In 1587 he became organist of Salisbury and was later organist of Hereford Cathedral. His son John was born at Salisbury in 1575. The D minor Service is a first-rate work on simple lines. It has *Jubilate* in the place of *Benedictus*, which was rather unusual at this period.

WILLIAM MUNDY, according to his pedigree,[4] was born *c.* 1530. He began as a chorister at Westminster Abbey, was a

---

[1] Both in *Tudor Church Music*, 8vo ed., No. 60.
[2] Tenbury, MS. 791. See p. 103, n. 5.
[3] *Tudor Church Music*, 8vo ed., Nos. 62 and 33. It was printed in G minor by Boyce.
[4] British Museum, Harl. 5580, fo. 20.

vicar-choral of St Paul's Cathedral from 1544 to 1564, and in
the latter year became a member of the Chapel Royal. He is
presumed to have died in 1591 since in that year another singer
took his place. He wrote a number of Latin motets but comparatively little music for the English rite. This, however,
included an elaborate service printed by Barnard in 1641,
consisting of *Venite, Te Deum, Benedictus, Kyrie, Credo, Magnificat*
and *Nunc dimittis*, and also five or six anthems. *O Lord, the
maker of all thing*,[1] still sung, is a smooth and tranquil setting of
words from the *King's Primer* of 1545, which suggests that it was
a comparatively early work. Two other anthems printed by
Barnard – *O Lord, the world's saviour* and *O Lord, I bow the knees* –
show the same quiet mastery. Morley mentions him among
a group of 'famous english men' which includes Taverner,
Sheppard, White and Byrd.[2]

It is not known in what year ROBERT PARSONS was born,
but as he was sworn a gentleman of the Chapel Royal in 1563
it is likely that he was under 30 at that date. In which case his
life was short, for he was drowned accidentally when bathing
in the Trent at Newark in 1570. In addition to Latin church
music he wrote as many as three services and a few anthems.
One of his services, including *Venite, Kyrie* and *Credo* in addition
to the morning and evening canticles, is in four, five, six and
seven parts; it was printed in Barnard's collection. *Venite* is one
of the most elaborate of all the settings of this psalm as a
canticle. The final phrases of the *Gloria* of *Nunc dimittis* in
this service are skilfully written in eight-part counterpoint.
Parsons' skill as a contrapuntist is again in evidence in his six-
part anthem *Deliver me from mine enemies*, in which the two treble
parts are in strict canon at the unison.

The anthem *Rejoice in the Lord always*,[3] traditionally ascribed
to JOHN REDFORD, would seem from its style and technique
to belong to the early Elizabethan period. It is a remarkably
polished little work, and it is difficult to believe that it could
date from the reign of Edward VI. At the same time it can

[1] *Tudor Church Music*, 8vo ed., No. 38.
[2] *A Plaine and Easie Introduction*, p. 151 (modern edition by R. A. Harman,
p. 255).
[3] *Tudor Church Music*, 8vo ed. No. 55.

hardly be later than 1563. The only known source is the so-called Mulliner book,[1] in which it occurs as an organ piece, with only the first five words of the text. Since Redford died in 1547[2] it is impossible that he could be the composer of the anthem, which is set to the English version of the Epistle for the fourth Sunday in Advent, as it first appeared in the Prayer Book of 1549. Furthermore the music is anonymous in the Mulliner book.

[1] British Museum, Add. 30,513, fo. 69ᵛ; *Musica Britannica*, i, ed. D. Stevens, p. 53. Thomas Mulliner was organist of Corpus Christi College, Oxford in 1563.

[2] A. W. Reed, *Early Tudor Drama* (1926), p. 55.

CHAPTER 6

William Byrd

It is a remarkable fact that the latter part of Elizabeth I's reign saw a significant development in music and literature which continued throughout the reign of James I (1603–25). This may in some measure have been due to an increased opportunity for cultivating the arts of peace after the destruction of the Spanish Armada in 1588. But such an explanation cannot wholly account for the appearance of so many men of exceptional genius. Shakespeare was born in 1564; Marlowe in the same year; Francis Bacon in 1561; John Donne and Ben Jonson in 1573. Among musicians, Morley was born in 1558; Dowland and Bull in 1562; Tomkins about 1572; Wilbye in 1574, and Weelkes about 1575.

WILLIAM BYRD (1543–1623) was by far the greatest figure in musical world of his time, not only by reason of his brilliant genius but also because at least fifty years of his long life were occupied in composition. Among the musicians of the later Elizabethan period he was by many years the senior; Morley, his pupil, was fifteen years younger. No wonder that the younger generation that included Weelkes, Wilbye, Tomkins and Gibbons looked up to him as a towering personality 'never without reverence to be named of the musicians'.[1] Except for the 'Psalmes' and other sacred pieces which Byrd included with his 'Sonets and Songs' and in his *Songes of sundrie natures*, all of which were printed in his own time and dated, it is not possible even approximately to say with certainty at what period any of his music for the English rite was composed. There is not, in fact, a very large quantity of it apart from the pieces in the published sets of 1588, 1589 and 1611; and this is not altogether

[1] Morley, *op. cit.*, p. 115 (modern edition, p. 202).

surprising when it is remembered that his sympathies throughout his life were with the Latin rite.

He was appointed organist and master of the choristers of
Lincoln Cathedral in 1563,[1] and held office there for nearly ten
years, after which he became a member of the Chapel Royal.
It may be conjectured that some of his settings of the canticles,
and possibly his *Preces and Responses*, Litany and *psalmi festivales*
belong to his time at Lincoln. His settings of the service were
numerous. The Short Service and the Great Service include
the morning and evening canticles and also *Venite*, *Kyrie* and
Credo. The second and third services are limited to *Magnificat*
and *Nunc dimittis*. A *Te Deum* and *Benedictus* in F major and a
Jubilate in G major are known today only from fragments.

Byrd wrote two versions of the *Preces* alone but only one of
the complete *Versicles and Responses*.[2] His setting of the response
'O Lord, make haste to help us' has become familiar because
it has been commonly substituted for the simpler setting by
Tallis, and it has erroneously appeared as the work of Tallis in
editions of the latter's Responses. Byrd's concluding phrase of
the *Gloria* in his second version of the *Preces* has also wrongly
found its way into Tallis in modern editions. The original text
of the two composers is as shown at the top of the next page.
Byrd's Litany[3] is a simple setting in four parts, with the plainsong in the tenor part. The alto part is missing, but it can easily
be reconstructed. It is remarkable that Byrd included the final
section that follows the Lesser Litany. It is extremely probable
that this belongs to his Lincoln period. The Psalms, however,
seem to be of later date, for in his treatment of *Teach me, O
Lord* (Ps. 119, vv. 33–8)[4] he broke new ground altogether. The
first, third and fifth verses are assigned to a solo voice, followed
in each instance by a verse for the full choir of five voices. The
composition opens with a short phrase for the organ alone, and
the solo voice is accompanied by an independent organ part.
This is probably one of the very earliest English experiments

[1] For the document of his appointment, dated 24 April, see Watkins Shaw,
'William Byrd of Lincoln', *Music & Letters*, xlviii (1967), p. 52.
  [2] *Tudor Church Music*, ii, pp. 3–4, 13–14, 45–8.
    [3] *Ibid.*, pp. 49–50.   [4] *Ibid.*, pp. 21–4.

in the employment of a solo voice in this manner. For the Ascension Day psalm, *Lift up your heads*,[1] Byrd introduced an English version of his Latin motet *Attollite portas*.[2] The motet was one of those included in the set of *Cantiones sacrae* which he published in partnership with Tallis in 1575. This fact supports the theory that these *psalmi festivales* belong to the later Elizabethan period.

It is likely that the Short Service[3] was produced at Lincoln. The terms 'short' and 'great' in relation to Elizabethan services correspond to 'simple' and 'elaborate'. The setting of the English canticles had its origin in the closing years of Henry VIII's reign, when simplicity was the keynote (see p. 38). Elizabethan composers felt able to treat the 'simple', or 'short', service which was still the usual model, with rather more freedom. On the other hand, they occasionally set the canticles in a more elaborate manner, giving fuller expression to their

---

[1] *Tudor Church Music*, ii, pp. 34–44.
[2] *Ibid.*, ix, pp. 92–8.   [3] *Ibid.*, ii, pp. 51–98.

interpretation of the words, and recognizing no restraint in repeating verbal phrases or in introducing short melismatic passages on a single syllable. These more elaborate settings came to be known as 'great' services.

Byrd's Short Service is a model of conciseness; it displays a subtle appreciation of the meaning of each sentence of the words and of the true verbal accentuation; it abounds in melodic interest and rhythmic variety, while the schemes of modulation and key-contrast show remarkable insight. Compared with Tallis's 'Dorian' Service and other works by Edwardian composers it is completely mature; and it remains unsurpassed to this day in its particular style as an unaccompanied service.

Venite is one of the best movements. It is unfortunate that, since it is impossible to go back on the age-long custom of singing this canticle to a chant, it can seldom be performed. Like Tallis, Byrd employed antiphonal treatment in repeating the phrases, in accordance with the traditional usage in choirs. Thus in the following passage he handled the musical material, both as to measure and rhythm, so as to make it fit neatly with the corresponding verbal phrase:

The opening of this movement is a joyous realization of the invitatory significance of the psalm:

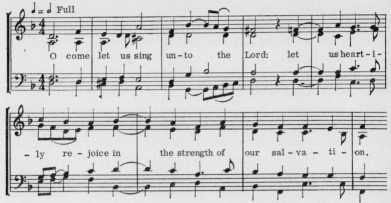

The Short Service consists of *Venite*, *Te Deum*, *Benedictus*, two *Kyries*, *Credo*, *Magnificat* and *Nunc dimittis*. Of these the *Credo* is the most elaborately developed, with certain passages in five and six parts. It was sung at the Coronation of King George VI. *Magnificat* is the outstanding movement, showing a recognizable scheme of modulation. The brilliant concluding bars of the Gloria may be especially noticed, with the tonic major chord used throughout the last three bars instead of being reserved for the final chord – a very effective touch:

A *Sanctus* assigned to this service in a late seventeenth-century manuscript[1] exists in the form of a skeleton organ score. There is no certainty that it is authentic.

The Great Service[2] seems to be a later composition. It is one of Byrd's best works, ranking with his Mass for five voices, and certainly the finest unaccompanied setting of the service in the entire repertory of English church music. It includes the usual morning and evening canticles, together with *Venite* and also *Kyrie* and *Credo*. Possibly it was written for some special occasion. This is all the more likely because the surviving text is extremely scarce, which suggests that it was found too long for general use. It was, however, certainly sung at Durham in the seventeenth century, otherwise it would not have been copied into the choir-books that still survive in the cathedral library. The settings of the *Gloria* in *Magnificat* and *Nunc dimittis* are both superb achievements. Developed at considerable length, they are unsurpassed examples of majestic polyphony. The concluding bars of *Nunc dimittis* are quoted here, showing how, after a full close in G major, the *Gloria* opens immediately on the chord of F major – a good example of key contrasts:

[1] British Museum, Add. 34,203, fo.8ᵛ.   [2] *Tudor Church Music*, ii, pp. 123–222.

Byrd's two other services, which are limited to the evening canticles, are certainly among his later works. The 'Second' Service[1] is constructed on what was quite a novel scheme at the close of the sixteenth century. It opens with a few bars of introduction for the organ, and the first phrase of the words is assigned to a solo voice. There are similar passages for solo voice with organ accompaniment during *Nunc dimittis* as well as in *Magnificat*. This work appears to be the earliest of the 'Verse' services, i.e. those in which one or more solo voices are employed with independent organ accompaniment to contrast with the passages sung by the full choir. The following extract will serve as an example:[2]

[1] *Tudor Church Music*, ii, pp. 99–110.
[2] The version printed here is from Ely Cathedral, MSS. 4 & 28. For another version see *Tudor Church Music*, ii, p. 103.

The *Gloria* of *Magnificat* includes a simple sequential treatment of the words 'and ever shall be':

Other Elizabethan and Jacobean composers followed Byrd's lead, notably Morley, Weelkes, Tomkins and Gibbons. It is therefore all the more surprising that none of their successful experiments should have been followed up after this period. It is curious that after the Jacobean period the Service, instead of advancing in interest and developing in form, remained unchanged and in many respects deteriorated. The Verse Service and the Great Service, even in a less extended form than Byrd's, had no successors of the same character for some two centuries. Rogers and Child in the mid-seventeenth century reverted to the Short Service. Even in the Restoration period, when the design of the anthem was changing from a motet into a cantata, the service remained tied to the short form. It is true that verse passages were introduced by many composers of Purcell's time, but these were written for solo voices in combination, not for a single voice. The chief pioneers in creating the modern service, with its independent organ part, its passages for solo voice, and verses for quartet or trio, were T. A. Walmisley and S. S. Wesley, who lived nearly three centuries later than Byrd.

Byrd's Third Service,[1] also for five voices, is obviously of later date than his Second. Being mainly in triple rhythm it was described by the copyist of an organ book at Christ Church, Oxford[2] as 'Mr. Bird's 3 minnoms'.

Many of Byrd's settings of sacred English texts were published in three sets of vocal compositions which include secular works: *Psalmes, Sonets, & songs of sadnes and pietie* (1588), *Songs of sundrie natures* (1589) and *Psalmes, Songs, and Sonnets* (1611).[3] A few also appeared in Sir William Leighton's anthology *Teares or Lamentacions of a Sorrowfull Soule* (1614). The 1588 and 1589 collections include a total of seventeen settings of metrical psalms. The words of one of these – *Lord, in thy wrath reprove me not* – are by Thomas Sternhold, of another – *O God, give ear and do apply* – by John Hopkins, his successor as editor of the 'Old Version' of the psalms. The authors of the remaining texts have not so far been identified. There is a difference in treatment between the 1588 settings and those in the 1589 collection. The 1588 psalms, like the rest of the pieces in the set, were originally written for solo voice with string accompaniment and include in each case several verses. The seven psalms in the 1589 collection, on the other hand, are for three voices, with only one verse printed. In both cases we may assume that these pieces were intended for private devotion: it is unlikely that they were ever sung in cathedrals. The melodic style is very closely based on that of the Anglo-Genevan tunes, as the following example (No. 8 of the 1588 set) will show:

---

[1] *Tudor Church Music*, ii, pp. 111–22.   [2] MS. 1001, fo. 42.
[3] *Collected Works*, xii–xiv = *The English Madrigalists*, xiv–xvi, ed. E. H. Fellowes, rev. ed. P. Brett & Thurston Dart.

How far the other sacred pieces in these collections were
designed for private performance must remain uncertain. It
would seem probable that all those in the 1588 collection,
being originally solo songs and having more than one verse,
were intended for domestic use; and the same applies to pieces
like *Have mercy upon me, O God* (1611, No. 25) and the carol
From virgin's womb (1589, Nos. 35 and 24), though both of these
involve a 'chorus'. Several of the settings for a group of voices
seem to fall into the same category, particularly those in only
three parts. With the remainder one cannot be certain, unless
there is actual evidence from cathedral part-books. It is significant that whereas Byrd's six-part *Sing joyfully* is found in several
manuscript sources as well as in Barnard's printed collection of

1641, his five-part *Sing we merrily* occurs only in *Psalmes, Songs, and Sonnets* (1611). Sometimes the mere difficulty of a setting may help as a criterion. The refrain of *From virgin's womb* would have severely taxed the resources of a cathedral choir, since there were normally very few boys:[1]

[1] It is arguable, from the disposition of the original clefs, that this was meant to sound a fourth lower, in which case it could be sung by four adult male voices.

In view of the fact that only a relatively small number of
cathedral part-books survive, the most we can do is to admit
that the two categories – the private anthem and the cathedral
anthem – sometimes overlapped.[1] In the case of *Have mercy
upon me, O God* there is positive evidence that they did: the piece
is found in cathedral sources with an organ accompaniment
instead of the original viol consort.

On cannot resist the impression that the sacred songs with
string accompaniment were closely modelled on secular songs
of the same kind – a form that was well established in the
choirboy plays of Elizabeth's reign.[2] Such pieces, in which the
strings weave a counterpoint about the voice, have a certain
squareness in the vocal line; and this characteristic is not
entirely absent from some of Byrd's sacred works for several
voices, e.g. *Turn our captivity* (1611, No. 30), though here the
squareness is relieved by the exuberant setting of the words
'But coming, they shall come with jollity':

[1] For a discussion of this question see P. le Huray, 'The English Anthem 1580–
1640', *Proceedings of the Royal Musical Association*, lxxxvi (1959–60), pp. 1–13.
[2] See [G. E. P. Arkwright], 'Early Elizabethan Stage Music', *The Musical
Antiquary*, 1909–10, pp. 30–40, and 1912–13, pp. 112–17.

On the other hand, where he was no longer shackled by an English text, as in the final Amen of *Praise our Lord, all ye Gentiles* (1611, No. 29):

Byrd could let his imagination flow as freely as in his Latin motets. It still remains true that the finest flowers of his genius are to be seen in his works for the Latin rite. It is not entirely an accident that one of his most loved works, *Bow thine ear*,[1] is an early adaptation of his motet *Civitas sancti tui* (*Sacrae Cantiones*, II, No. 21).[2]

[1] *Tudor Church Music*, 8vo ed., No. 61.
[2] *Collected Works*, ii.

CHAPTER 7

Morley and Tomkins

Although Byrd was the most venerable figure among English musicians at the close of the sixteenth century, THOMAS MORLEY (1557–1602), his junior by some fifteen years, was also a much older man than Wilbye, Weelkes, Tomkins and Gibbons. It is unfortunate that his fame as a madrigalist has tended to overshadow his important work as a church musician. He was master of the choristers at Norwich Cathedral from 1583 to 1587,[1] and in 1588 took the degree of B.Mus. at Oxford. Shortly after this he became organist of St Paul's Cathedral, and in 1592 he was appointed a gentleman of the Chapel Royal, continuing to hold office at St Paul's. His health was already failing in 1597, in which year his treatise *A Plaine and Easie Introduction to Practicall Musicke* was published. In the last ten years of his life his output of published works was exceptionally large. It included *Canzonets . . . to three voyces* in 1593, *Madrigalls to foure voyces* in 1595, *Balletts to five voyces* in 1595, *Canzonets to two voyces* in 1595, *Canzonets . . . to five and six voices* in 1597, a collection of Italian canzonets in 1597, a collection of madrigals by Italian composers in 1598, consort lessons 'by divers exquisite authors' in 1599, a book of airs (lute-songs) in 1600 and *The Triumphes of Oriana*, which he edited, in 1601.

These works must have absorbed most of his time throughout this period, especially as he spent some of it instructing pupils. Nevertheless, his compositions for the Church are by no means negligible. He seems to have been at one time a Catholic, which explains the fact that he wrote several Latin motets. Only a handful of English anthems have survived. Two of these are

---

[1] Watkins Shaw, 'Thomas Morley of Norwich', *Musical Times*, cvi (1965), pp. 669–73.

especially to be noticed: a full anthem, and one for solo and chorus. The full anthem opens with the Latin words *Nolo mortem peccatoris*, breaking into English: *Father, I am thine only Son.*[1] It is an intercessory subject very suitable for use on Good Friday. The opening words recur as a refrain. The composer has treated his subject with a profound feeling of reverence and pathos. The verse anthem *Out of the deep*[2] has alternate sections for solo and chorus. Morley's appreciation of the rhythm and accentuation of the words is admirably expressed in the opening solo:

_____

[1] *Tudor Church Music*, 8vo ed., No. 13.

[2] *Ibid.*, No. 71. To be distinguished from the six-part full anthem (an English adaptation of the composer's *De profundis*) which opens with the same words.

Morley wrote at least four services. The service described by
Barnard as his 'First' includes *Venite*, *Kyrie* and *Credo*, and the
usual morning and evening canticles.[1] It is a verse service, a
form which, in contrast to the polyphonic Short Service, had
become generally established by the close of the century.
Morley's treatment of this form showed some advance upon
Byrd's, for besides the employment of solo song with organ
accompaniment he introduced passages for duet, trio and a
quartet of solo voices. *Magnificat* in this setting begins with the
organ alone; the opening words are assigned to a single voice,
and the remainder of the first verse is written in contrapuntal
fashion for a quartet.

Morley wrote another service for the morning and evening
canticles, with *Kyrie* and *Credo*. This is a full service for five
voices. The text of it survives only in the Durham Cathedral
manuscripts and certain parts are missing. There are two other
settings of his of the evening canticles, one in four parts and one
in five. These are simpler in character; both of them should
be found useful in the modern cathedral repertory. The four-
part work[2] is very straightforward in design; imitative phrases
are introduced in well-varied contrast to the simpler homophonic passages, and both canticles end with an *Amen* in
imitative counterpoint. The five-part setting[3] is the simpler of the
two. The greater part of it is treated homophonically, but with
plenty of variety in the interchange of rhythm. The final *Amen*
of *Nunc dimittis* shows an effective use of changing-note groups:

---

[1] Evening canticles in *Tudor Church Music*, 8vo ed., No. 64.
[2] Ed. C. F. Simkins (Oxford University Press).
[3] Ed. R. G. Greening & H. K. Andrews (Stainer & Bell).

Morley's setting of the Burial Service[1] in the English Prayer
Book is the earliest of such works, although it was followed very
shortly by that of John Parsons, organist of Westminster Abbey
for less than two years before his death in 1623. Both these
settings seem to have been in general use throughout the seventeenth century. Parsons's was sung in Westminster Abbey at the
funeral of Charles II. Morley's setting retained its popularity
in the eighteenth century, as is shown by the fact that Boyce
included it in his *Cathedral Music*. It was sung at the funeral
of George II. For many years it has been superseded by the
use of Croft's beautiful setting of the opening sentences, while
the other passages in the service available for musical setting
have been treated by numerous composers from Purcell down to
modern times. Morley's service is the most complete of all the
settings, because it includes *Man that is born of a woman*, *Thou
knowest*, *Lord* and *I heard a voice from heaven* in addition to the
opening sentences. Burney[2] singled out the following passage
in *Thou knowest*, *Lord* as being 'extremely beautiful in the three
essentials of good Music: melody, harmony, and accent':

He also noted with appreciation 'the flat 6th given to G, when
the ear is habituated to expect a 5th', in the following passage
from *I heard a voice*:

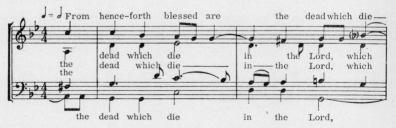

<hr />

[1] Ed. B. Rainbow (Novello). [2] *A General History of Music*, iii, p. 105.

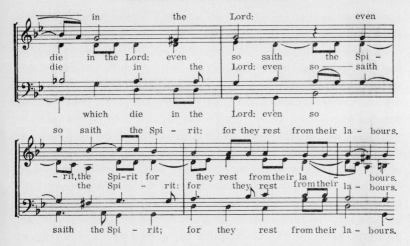

A setting of the *Preces and Responses* and also some *psalmi fes-tivales* are among Morley's other compositions for the Church. His prestige among musicians at the close of his comparatively short life was second only to that of his master, Byrd. A decade later Thomas Ravenscroft wrote of him[1] that 'he did shine as the Sun in the Firmament of our Art'.

THOMAS TOMKINS (1572–1656), like Morley, was a pupil of Byrd. He was born at St David's. The year of his birth is known from the fact that he was 78 on 17 June 1650,[2] on which date the Mayor and Aldermen of Worcester certified him to be 'an honest quiet peaceable man conformable to all orders and ordinances of Parliament'. They added that he had lived in Worcester 'very neare 60 yeares'. He belonged to a musical family: several of his brothers were musicians of some distinction. His earliest experiences of church music were at St David's Cathedral, where he was a chorister during the time that his father was organist. In 1596 he succeeded Nathaniel Pattrick, a promising musician who died young, as organist of Worcester Cathedral. He took the degree of B.Mus. at Oxford in 1607. He became a member of the Chapel Royal some time before 1620, but retained his position at Worcester until 1646 when, owing to the Civil War, the services at the cathedral were suspended.

[1] *A Briefe Discourse* (1614).
[2] P.R.O., Domestic State Papers, Interregnum, Vol. G. 124, No. 273.

He retired to Martin-Hussingtree in Worcestershire, where he died at a great age.

Tomkins's secular vocal work places him among the best of the English madrigal-composers, and his chamber-music for strings is also of very high merit and originality. He was one of the most prolific of all composers of English church music. Almost all of his sacred compositions were printed in a posthumous publication (1668) entitled *Musica Deo Sacra & Ecclesiae Anglicanae: or Musick Dedicated To the Honor and Service of God, and To the Use of Cathedral and other Churches of England.* It is in five volumes, four of which are voice-parts, one each for a part, while the fifth volume is the *Pars Organica*, or organ part. In this last are found the independent accompaniments to the solo voice-parts in the verse anthems, in addition to the kind of incomplete sketch of the vocal score that is usually found in the manuscript organ-books of the period. *Musica Deo Sacra* includes five services and 93 anthems, 41 of which are verse anthems. In the course of his long life Tomkins passed through a period of great change and development in the style and design of English church music, greatly influenced, as it was, by the dramatic and harmonic innovations made by Italian composers early in the seventeenth century. It is often said with a good deal of truth that the year 1600 marks the dividing line between ancient and modern music. In England there was no dividing line. English composers profited rather slowly by Italian innovations, and with a characteristically English genius for compromise incorporated them in their own tradition.

The work of Tomkins and of his contemporaries, such as Weelkes and Gibbons, seems to show that the drift towards the verse anthem did not become pronounced for another fifteen or twenty years. Tomkins, it may be supposed, wrote a large proportion of his full anthems in his earlier years at Worcester when he was still a young man and under the influence of such great masters of polyphony as Tallis, Byrd, Palestrina and Orlando di Lasso. It was in this older fashion that he chiefly excelled. There are few of his verse anthems which can be placed in the same class. Among the best is the Christmas anthem *Behold I bring you glad tidings*; but the outstanding feature of that composition is the ten-part chorus *Glory to God* rather than the verse section. Tomkins was undoubtedly at his best when writing for an exceptionally large number of parts. His setting of Psalm 117, *O praise the Lord, all ye heathen*,[1] for twelve voices is a magnificent example of contrapuntal skill employed with fine artistic inspiration. The climax at the words 'and the truth of the Lord' is masterly; and a wonderful independence of part-writing is displayed in all the voices. This same collection includes settings of collects for the great festivals and certain saints' days and two coronation anthems: *Be strong and of good courage* for James I, and *O Lord, grant the King a long life* for Charles I.

A feature of the verse anthems is the use of what might be called 'fragmented' sections for a group of solo voices, which imitate each other, either by overlapping or in close succession. This might easily result in a disjointed structure, but in fact the organ accompaniment supplies the necessary continuity. There are, however, examples of extended solos for a single voice – for example, in *Above the stars my saviour dwells*,[2] which opens as follows:

---

[1] *Tudor Church Music*, 8vo ed., No. 100.
[2] *Early English Church Music*, ix, No. 14.

The rhythm of the first bar for the organ is characteristic. One notices also how the vocal line is influenced both by the rhythm and by the melodic idiom of the metrical psalm. There are no harmonic surprises here. Tomkins is more adventurous in this excerpt for the full choir from *Almighty God, whose praise this day*:[1]

[1] *Early English Church Music*, v, No. 4.

As many as five services were printed in *Musica Deo Sacra*.[1]
Two more services survive in manuscript, but the text of these
is incomplete. The most important of the services is the third.
It includes *Te Deum, Jubilate, Magnificat* and *Nunc dimittis*, and
it is constructed in a very elaborate manner on the lines of a
Great Service (it was so styled in the 'Batten' organ book,[2]
though no such title is given to it in *Musica Deo Sacra*). The
morning canticles are on a bigger scale than *Magnificat* and
Nunc dimittis; several of the sections are in ten real parts. The
fourth service consists of no more than *Te Deum* and the two
usual evening canticles. This also is a verse service with passages
for solo voices as well as for quartet and trio. It opens with the
traditional intonation, assigned to the alto voices in full. Contrary to tradition it is accompanied in a curious manner with
the intonation introduced contrapuntally:

[1] *Tudor Church Music* viii.   [2] Tenbury, MS. 791, fo. 160.

G

It is evident that Tomkins understood the plan upon which *Te Deum* is constructed as a hymn of praise, originally ending with the phrase 'in glory everlasting', for he closes this phrase with a fine passage in eight-part imitative counterpoint, and follows it with a solo voice throughout the next verse. *Vouchsafe, O Lord* is also assigned to a solo voice, with the chorus responding.

The opening phrase of *Magnificat* is identical with that of Byrd's Second Service. Tomkins's accompaniment, however, is considerably more elaborate:

Other passages in this service show a similar elaboration. For example, the solo voice at the words 'O Lord, in thee have I trusted' in *Te Deum*, is accompanied thus:

This kind of elaboration occurs also in the writing for solo voices in the verse anthems – for instance, in *Above the stars my saviour dwells*, where the singer appears to be imitating the organ:

*eyes

A curious mannerism in Tomkins's work is his habit of frequently repeating the final tag of a verbal phrase. For example, in his anthem *Great and marvellous* the first sentence

ends with the repetition of the two words 'thy works'. A few
bars later the voices are singing 'True and just are thy ways,
thy ways'. Another anthem opens with the phrase 'O God,
wonderful art thou, art thou'. The same mannerism is found in
his secular work. On the other hand he shows a just appreciation of the value of words. One might cite *O Lord, grant the
king a long life*,[1] where the word 'long' stands out from the
rest of the phrase by being twice given four beats, or *Almighty
God, which hast knit together*,[2] where the phrase 'to those un-
speakable joys' is given point by a lively syncopation which
places the emphasis firmly on the second syllable of 'un-
speakable'.

Tomkins's First Service is a fairly simple Short Service for
four voices. It includes *Venite*, *Kyrie* and *Credo* and his only
setting of *Benedictus*. He set *Jubilate* by preference in three of his
five services, and in his Fourth Service he set *Te Deum* alone
without either *Benedictus* or *Jubilate*. The Second Service is also
in the form of a Short Service for four voices, including the
same numbers, except that *Jubilate* replaces *Benedictus*. The Fifth
is another verse service. It is the least satisfactory of the five;
the large proportion of verse passages results in a disjointed
effect. *Musica Deo Sacra* also includes a setting of the *Preces and
Responses* and part of the Burial Service, but the words of the
opening sentences do not exactly follow the text of the Prayer
Book.

The *Pars Organica* of this work includes the statement[3] that
the semibreve is to be measured by two beats of the human
pulse, or of a pendulum two feet in length, and that the note F,
on the fourth line of the bass stave, was that produced by an
open pipe two and a half feet in length. As to the first point:
the speed indicated – roughly equivalent in metronomic terms
to $\mathord{\downharpoonleft} = 76$[4] – would probably now be considered too slow, except where there is a good deal of figuration; moreover it is
difficult to believe that all Tomkins's music should be performed at a uniform speed. The second point is of more

---

[1] *Early English Church Music*, v, No. 8.   [2] *Ibid.*, No. 11.
[3] Only in the Tenbury copy. The author is presumably Tomkins's son Nathaniel.
[4] In modern editions, with reduced note-values, $\mathord{\downharpoonleft} = 76$.

importance, for it suggests that the pitch of church music at that time was nearly a minor third higher than it now is; and this may be held to justify the transposition of sixteenth-century church music in modern editions to keys a minor third higher than those indicated in the original text. It should be emphasized that the note about pitch refers exclusively to music for church choirs. Secular vocal music was written and printed at a pitch that corresponds to modern pitch, except where the clefs used indicate downward transposition. The pitch of organs, on the other hand, was considerably higher than choir pitch,[1] which meant that organists, unless they had transposed parts, had to transpose down when accompanying.

[1] i.e. assuming that the 5 ft principal is taken as the norm. If the 10 ft open diapason is the standard, the organ pitch was lower than choir pitch and transposition up was necessary. For a detailed discussion see P. le Huray, *Music and the Reformation in England, 1549–1660* (1967), pp. 112–15.

CHAPTER 8

Weelkes and Gibbons

It is strange that so great a madrigal-writer as John Wilbye should have composed almost nothing for the Church. The two short pieces contributed to Leighton's *Teares and Lamentacions* can scarcely have been intended as anthems, and these represent all that is known of his sacred compositions. His contemporary THOMAS WEELKES (d. 1623) was, by contrast, one of the outstanding church musicians at the beginning of the seventeenth century.

He was born three or four years after Tomkins. He is first heard of as organist of Winchester College in the closing years of the sixteenth century, having been appointed about the end of 1598. Before that date he had already published his first set of madrigals in 1597. He took the degree of B.Mus. at Oxford in 1602 and became organist of Chichester Cathedral. In spite of his irresponsible behaviour and drunkenness he held this post until his death in London. He was buried at St Bride's Church, Fleet Street.

As a madrigal-writer he was supreme. In his cathedral music he was far more reserved; but the same power and perfection of technique in handling a chorus of six or more voices is displayed. Since he died before reaching the age of 50 his output of church music is considerable in relation to the length of his life. He wrote more services than any of the other Tudor composers; as many as nine are known, but none of these has survived with its text complete. It is possible to reconstruct four out of the nine, and the surviving text of the remaining five is enough to demonstrate that Weelkes was the most original and perhaps the greatest of all the English composers of services at this time with the possible exception of Byrd. The following is a list:

1. First Service 'to the organs in Gamut' (also described as 'with verse for a meane'): *Te Deum, Jubilate,* Offertory (*Blessed is he*), *Kyrie, Credo, Magnificat, Nunc dimittis.*
2. Second Service 'to the organs in D sol re': *Te Deum, Jubilate,* Offertory (*Blessed be the man*), *Kyrie, Credo, Magnificat, Nunc dimittis.*
3. *Magnificat* and *Nunc dimittis* 'to the organs in F fa ut'.
4. Service 'for trebles': *Te Deum, Magnificat, Nunc dimittis.*
5. *Magnificat* and *Nunc dimittis* 'in medio chori'.
6. *Magnificat* and *Nunc dimittis* 'in verse for 2 contratenors'.
7. Service in four parts: *Venite, Te Deum, Jubilate, Magnificat, Nunc dimittis.*
8. Service in five parts: *To Deum, Jubilate, Magnificat, Nunc dimittis.*
9. *Magnificat* and *Nunc dimittis* in seven parts.

A study of these services, even in their incomplete text, reveals the extent of Weelkes's inventive genius in exploring fresh methods and developing the design, especially with the object of adding interest and variety to this class of composition. The position to which he advanced this branch of music was not reached again until the latter part of the nineteenth century. In his own day, and for a while after his death, these services evidently enjoyed a wide popularity. It is remarkable that as many as six of them were included in the so-called 'Batten' organ book. The four-part service (No. 7) is an attractive setting designed on the simple lines of a full Short Service. The reconstruction of the alto part, much of which is missing in the manuscripts, presents no great difficulty. The five-part service (No. 8) is also in Short Service form. The organ score in this instance is unusually full, so that it has been possible to reconstruct the evening canticles with a fair measure of satisfaction.[1] In character this service is definitely madrigalian as compared with other Tudor and Jacobean settings, in that almost every phrase is written with points of imitation. On the other hand, the madrigalian manner of repeating short verbal phrases two or three times is not followed; it would obviously be unsuited

---

[1] *Tudor Church Music,* 8vo ed., No. 96.

to such a subject. The drop of a seventh in all the parts in the phrase 'he hath put down the mighty' is characteristic of Weelkes' originality, especially as the interval is actually a major seventh in the bass and alto parts. The *Gloria* in both these canticles is superbly set. The beautiful *Amen* of *Magnificat*:

also occurs, in a modified form, at the end of the anthem *O how amiable*.[1]

---

[1] *Musica Britannica*, xxiii, pp. 35–9.

The most elaborate of these services is that described as 'for trebles' (No. 4), so called because the full sections include a high soprano part. There are many fine choral effects in this composition; in certain places the music is laid out for double-choir of five voices – for instance, in *Magnificat* at 'and holy is his name', and again, 'as he promised'. In *Nunc dimittis* the phrase 'according to thy word' is in ten parts. Weelkes must have had a large choir in mind when he wrote this work; there are four independent parts for boys' voices in certain passages. It may have been written for some special occasion. Certainly in general character and design it is unique in the repertory of cathedral music.[1]

The Evening Service No. 5 is described as 'in medio chori'. Certain services by other composers are so described in early seventeenth-century manuscripts. The meaning of the term has baffled musicians and liturgiologists alike. It evidently indicates the employment of solo voices in some manner; but it is not identical in meaning with the term 'verse', which is sometimes found in contrast to it in the same composition. Neither, for a similar reason, has it any relation to the terms *Decani*, *Cantoris* or *Full*. It may be that a small group of solo singers was placed beyond the choir-stalls in the centre of the space nearer to the sanctuary, that is to say *in medio chori*. Interesting effects could certainly have been produced in such a manner, but a larger body of voices than the usual complement of a cathedral choir would then need to have been employed. Weelkes's genius for massive choral writing also prompted him to compose an Evening Service in seven parts (No. 9). This has survived complete apart from the tenor part.

More than 40 anthems by this composer are known,[2] but the text of many of them is incomplete. Seeing that Weelkes wrote so much fine church music, it is extraordinary that so much of it should have passed into oblivion. Barnard[3] included no more than one of his anthems (*O Lord, grant the king a long life*) and none of his services. Boyce[4] neglected him entirely. His greatest

---

[1] Evening Service, ed. P. le Huray (Stainer & Bell).
[2] Those surviving virtually complete are in *Musica Britannica*, xxiii.
[3] *Selected Church Music* (1641). [4] *Cathedral Music* (1760–78).

anthem is *Hosanna to the Son of David*. This makes very interesting comparison with the setting of the same subject by Orlando Gibbons. Both reach the highest level of polyphonic writing. Weelkes's treatment is the more massive of the two; this point is especially in evidence near the end, where all the voices together shout *Hosanna* twice in a clear-cut phrase, in a manner suggesting that the crowd had halted and joined in a united cry of welcome. Gibbons's treatment suggests rather that the crowd

was in hurried movement, calling out their *Hosannas* independently but with unrestrained enthusiasm. *Gloria in excelsis:
Sing my soul* is written in a massive style somewhat similar to
Hosanna. It is a brilliant anthem for a festival, more particularly
for Christmas, with a splendidly solid opening, shown opposite,
which is recapitulated before the final *Amen. O Lord, arise* is an
elaborate work for seven voices, which begins, quietly, works up
to a vivid setting of 'and thy saints sing with joyfulness', and
ends with an intricate *Alleluia.*[1]

Of the few verse anthems that survive the majority appear to
come into the category of sacred songs with accompaniment,
even though they include choruses. It is arguable, however, that
O Lord, how joyful is the king was sung in church as a thanksgiving
after the Gunpowder Plot, since it is described as for the 'Fift
of November'. The melodic interest of the voice parts in these
pieces is relatively slight: the organ parts are on the whole more
enterprising. The style of the solos is not unlike that of Byrd's
psalm settings, which is not surprising, as the texts of several of
them are taken from metrical versions. The opening of *Plead
thou my cause* may serve as an example:

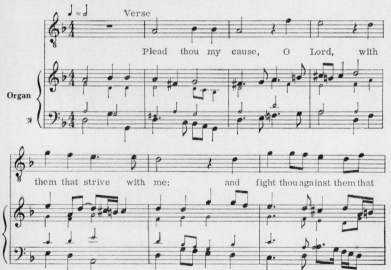

[1] The anthem *Let thy merciful ears*, sometimes attributed to Weelkes, is by John
Mudd.

ORLANDO GIBBONS (1583–1625), born in Oxford, was the youngest and last of the great Elizabethans. Some notable English musicians did in fact survive him; Wilbye lived till 1638, but he wrote nothing that is known after 1614. Other madrigalists and lutenists were still living in 1625, but for the most part their work was already finished. Tomkins and some of the lesser church musicians lived for several years after this date, but fashions were changing. The Italians had pointed the way in a new direction towards opera and oratorio, and towards solo music, both vocal and instrumental. England was shortly to be harassed with civil warfare, and church music, apart from metrical psalms, was to be banned altogether. Gibbons's early death virtually marks the end of a distinguished period of cathedral music.

He had his first training as a church musician at King's College, Cambridge, where he became a chorister in 1596 at the age of 12, under the direction of his brother Edward. He was appointed organist of the Chapel Royal in 1605, but it was not until 1623 that he became organist of Westminster Abbey. He died suddenly on 5 June 1625 at Canterbury, where with the rest of the Chapel Royal he was in attendance on Charles I and his Court. The King had come to Canterbury for the purpose of awaiting the arrival of his queen, Henrietta Maria, at Dover. The marriage had taken place in Paris on 1 May, the king being presented by proxy. The queen arrived at Canterbury on Sunday, 12 June, exactly a week after Gibbons's death.

Gibbons's set of madrigals was published in 1612. In comparison with those of Morley, Wilbye and Weelkes, they are far more austere both in subject and in treatment. They should be studied in relation to his anthems, for, unlike the work of other madrigal-composers who were also church musicians, there is less difference of style and character between his treatment of the two forms. He wrote about 40 anthems,[1] as many as two-thirds of which are verse anthems. His full anthems *Hosanna to the Son of David*, *Lift up your hands* and *O clap your hands* are among the greatest religious songs of praise of all time. The last-named, together with its second section *God is gone up*, is a particularly noble work for double choir.

In certain early manuscripts the opening passage of *Hosanna to the Son of David* is assigned to solo voices; the full choir enters at 'Blessed is he'. The effect thus produced suggests the presence

---

[1] *Tudor Church Music*, iv. Verse anthems also in *Early English Church Music*, iii. The following complete anthems printed in *Tudor Church Music* are by other composers: *Have mercy upon me* is from Byrd's *Psalmes, Songs, and Sonnets* (1611), and *O Lord increase our faith* and *Why art thou so heavy* are by Henry Loosemore.

of only a few people at the opening scene, swelling later into a crowd enthusiastically acclaiming the Saviour. Gibbons made a kind of conflate of three sentences from the Gospels: 'Blessed is he that cometh in the name of the Lord'; 'Blessed be the king of Israel', and 'Blessed be the kingdom [of David] that cometh in the name of the Lord'. The concluding section recapitulates some of the music of the opening. In contrast to the vigour of this setting *O Lord, in thy wrath,* for six voices, is a work of a penitential character, expressing perfectly the profound feelings of a sorrowful soul. The following moving phrase, in which one of the treble voices is silent, comes after a close in D minor:

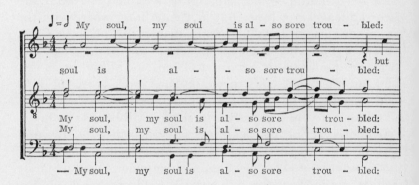

It is evident from the large number of Gibbons's verse anthems that he took pleasure in experimenting with this relatively new form. Several of them have accompaniment for strings in place of the organ, and this gives greater clarity to the polyphony. In his writing for solo voices Gibbons shows himself sensitive to the niceties of the English text. The solo sections of *This is the record of John* furnish illustrations of splendid declamatory phrasing, e.g.:

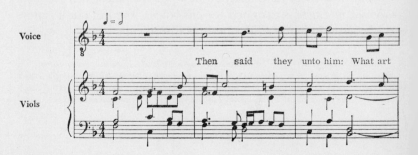

thou? That we may give, that we may give an answer unto them that sent us. What sayest thou of thy-self? And he said: I am the voice of him that cri-eth in the wil--der-ness: Make straight the way of the Lord, make straight the way of the Lord, the way of the Lord.

Equally effective is this passage from *Behold, thou hast made my days*:

O God, the king of glory has a very effective drop of a seventh in the bass and treble voice-parts in the final phrase:

Gibbons's Short Morning and Evening Service in F major has never lost its popularity. It has a striking individuality and in spite of its often complex texture (the *Gloria* of *Nunc dimittis* includes a canon for treble and alto) the clarity of the words never seems to be obscured. The *Kyrie* and *Credo* of this service are seldom sung. The *Sanctus* sometimes included is an adaptation from phrases in *Te Deum* dating from the end of the seventeenth century. The verse service is not quite on the same high level: the solo passages seem rather too numerous and disjointed in *Te Deum*. But the evening canticles, both ending with the same fine Amen, are very effective. Gibbons also set *Preces* and special psalms to music for Easter Day and Whit-Sunday in the festal manner of the period. His seventeen hymn-tunes,[1] though not designed for cathedral use, form a valuable contribution to English church music.

[1] *Tudor Church Music*, iv, pp. 317–24.

CHAPTER 9

Lesser Elizabethan, Jacobean and Caroline Composers

This chapter will deal briefly with the work of the lesser composers of church music in the period that extends from the closing years of the sixteenth century until the outbreak of the Civil War. The term 'lesser composers' is intended to refer exclusively to their church music, for some of them achieved far greater distinction as madrigalists or in the field of instrumental music. Some 30 of these composers call for mention here, and it will be convenient to take them in alphabetical order.

RICHARD ALISON concluded his book of madrigals (1606), quaintly entitled *An Howres Recreation in Musicke*,[1] with two anthems and a sacred song. The first of the anthems is a well-written piece in madrigalian style, *Behold now, praise the Lord*. It works up to a good climax at the words 'give thee blessing out of Sion', followed by a fine extended *Amen*. He had previously published in 1599 a psalter for domestic use entitled *The Psalmes of David in Meter, The plaine Song being the common tunne to be sung and plaide upon the Lute, Orpharyon, Citterne or Base Violl, severally or altogether, the singing part to be either Tenor or Treble to the Instrument, according to the nature of the voyce, or for fowre voyces. With tenne short Tunnes in the end, to which for the most part all the Psalmes may be usually sung.* . . . Alison had previously had experience in this branch of work, having been a contributor to East's *Whole Booke of Psalmes* in 1592. His psalter was one of the earliest in which the melody was placed in the treble part. It has been described[2] as the best of all the works of this kind, although it was severely criticized by Burney.[3]

---

[1] *The English Madrigalists*, xxxiii.
[2] *Grove's Dictionary of Music and Musicians* (5th ed.), vi, p. 967, n. 2.
[3] *A General History of Music*, iii, p. 57.

JOHN AMNER (d. 1641) became organist of Ely Cathedral in 1610 in succession to George Barcroft, and was ordained deacon in 1617. He composed at least three services, for the third is so described in the manuscripts.[1] His *Preces and Psalms* for Christmas Eve, and also a *Gloria in excelsis*, are among the manuscripts at Peterhouse. He wrote a large number of anthems, but the surviving text of those that remain in manuscript is very defective. A collection of 26 short pieces, which he described as *Sacred Hymns of 3, 4, 5 and 6 parts for Voices and Vyols* was published in 1615: it is clearly intended for domestic use, presumably in the house of the Earl of Bath, to whom it is affectionately dedicated.

THOMAS BATESON (d. 1630) was famous as a madrigal-composer. In spite of his position as a cathedral organist, first at Chester and later in Dublin, only one anthem of his is known, *Holy Lord God Almighty*,[2] which he wrote for seven voices. A service by him is said to have been sung in Chester Cathedral until the beginning of the nineteenth century, but no text of it is now known.

Little is known of the early life of ADRIAN BATTEN (d. 1637). He was a pupil of John Holmes, organist of Winchester Cathedral, and became a lay-clerk at Westminster Abbey in 1614. Subsequently he became organist of St Paul's Cathedral in 1624. His output of cathedral music was among the largest of his contemporaries. There seem to have been as many as nine or ten services, one of which was described as his 'long' service,[3] a term that presumably meant the same thing as a Great Service. More than 50 anthems by this composer survive. A number of these are available in modern editions. Batten's achievement was modest, but his relatively simple anthems, such as *Haste thee, O God* and *Deliver us, O Lord our God*[4] are by no means to be despised.[5]

---

[1] Peterhouse, Durham and York.   [2] Ed. J. F. Fitzgerald (Novello).
[3] Christ Church, Oxford, MSS. 1220–4.
[4] *Tudor Church Music*, 8vo ed., Nos. 78 and 56.
[5] Tenbury MS. 791, a volume of nearly 1,000 pages consisting of anthems and services, is commonly refered to as 'Batten's Organ Book', but there is no evidence that he was the compiler; see P. le Huray, 'Towards a Definitive Study of Pre-Restoration Anglican Service Music', *Musica Disciplina*, xiv (1960), pp. 172–6.

ELWAY BEVIN, according to Anthony Wood,[1] was organist of Bristol Cathedral from 1589 to 1638. It is assumed that he died shortly after that date, since in Archbishop Laud's visitation of 1634[2] he is described as a 'verie olde man'. He was a distinguished theorist, and published a *Briefe and Short Instruction of the Art of Musicke* (1631). He wrote at least three services, one of which, in the Dorian mode, still holds a well-merited place in cathedral choirs. His few anthems have passed into oblivion.

JOHN BULL (*c.* 1562–1628) is one of the most distinguished musicians of this period, but his fame rests upon his rare skill both as a composer and as a performer of works for keyboard instruments. He wrote very little church music, but two of his anthems enjoyed great popularity in his day; they were familiarly known as 'the Starr anthem', and 'the Roringe anthem', being so styled in several early manuscripts. The first of these was the Epiphany collect, *Almighty God, who by the leading of a star*.[3] It was re-arranged by Aldrich and printed in Boyce's *Cathedral Music*[4] as *O Lord, my God*. The second, *In thee, O Lord*, includes the verse 'I have roared for the very disquietness of my heart'. The treatment of this passage is so grotesque that it would be impossible to sing it in church at the present time.

WILLIAM CRANFORD was a lay-clerk of St Paul's Cathedral in the reign of Charles I. A service and several anthems by him are included in the 'Batten' organ book; one or two more are among the Durham and Peterhouse manuscripts. They evidently had a vogue at the time.

RICHARD DERING (d. 1630) was organist to Queen Henrietta Maria in the reign of Charles I. As a Roman Catholic he naturally wrote little for the English rites, but one or two anthems survive in manuscript.

MICHAEL EAST (d. 1648) was probably son of Thomas East, the publisher of many of the English madrigal sets. His interest as a composer was mainly in madrigals, of which he produced

---

[1] *Fasti Oxonienses*, ed. P. Bliss, ii, p. 265.
[2] *Historical Manuscripts Commission*, Report IV (1874), p. 141.
[3] *Tudor Church Music*, 8vo ed., No. 91.
[4] Vol. III.

two sets,[1] as well as two miscellaneous collections,[2] two books of instrumental music, and a set of verse anthems.[3] The two miscellaneous collections (Books III and IV) include anthems as well as secular pieces. One of the best of these is *Turn thy face from my wickedness* (Book III), which has a lively *Amen* at the end of the second part:

---

[1] *The English Madrigalists,* xxix and xxx.
[2] *Ibid.,* xxxi[a] and xxxi[b].   [3] *Musical Antiquarian Society,* xiv.

In general these works suffer from a certain stiffness. An evening service is among the Peterhouse manuscripts. East was organist of Lichfield Cathedral from about 1618 until his death. Thomas East compiled and issued *The Whole Booke of Psalmes: with their wonted Tunes, as they are song in Churches, composed into foure parts* (1592). For the four-part settings ten composers were chosen, among whom were John Farmer, George Kirbye, Richard Alison, Giles Farnaby, John Dowland and Edmund Hooper. Four entirely new tunes were added. Three of these were given the names 'Glassenburie', 'Kentish' and 'Cheshire'. 'Kentish' was known later as 'Rochester'. The fourth had no name but was afterwards called 'Winchester'.

ALFONSO FERRABOSCO (*c.* 1575–1628), who was born at Greenwich, may be considered an English composer. His father, as recorded by Morley,[1] entered into friendly contention with Byrd in writing canons on the plainsong *Miserere*. His sons were also musicians: one of them, John, became organist of Ely Cathedral. Alfonso contributed three pieces to Leighton's *Teares or Lamentacions*. An anthem, *Have ye no regard*, is in the 'Batten' organ book. His book of lute-songs published in 1609 includes a number of lyrics by Ben Jonson. His chief distinction as a composer was in the field of instrumental chamber music.

THOMAS FORD (d. 1648) was one of the great group of English lute-song composers. He was the exact contemporary of Michael East and died in the same year. His anthems *Almighty God, who hast me brought*[2] and *In thee, O Lord, I put my trust* were included in Leighton's *Teares or Lamentacions*. There are also several pieces for three voices.[3]

NATHANIEL GILES (d. 1634) was a long-lived musician whose works cannot be approximately dated. He came of musical stock: his father was organist of St Paul's Cathedral. He became organist of Worcester Cathedral in 1581, and four years later one of the organists of St George's Chapel, Windsor. He was evidently a successful choir-master, for it is recorded that when the Duke of Württemberg visited Windsor in 1592 he noted

---

[1] *A Plaine and Easie Introduction to Practicall Musicke*, p. 115.
[2] Ed. J. E. West (Novello).
[3] Christ Church, Oxford, MSS. 736–8.

that 'the music and especially the organ was very fine', and that 'a boy sang so beautifully that it was wonderful to hear him'.[1] Giles wrote two verse services including *Te Deum*, *Jubilate*, *Kyrie* and *Credo* and the evening canticles, besides two more evening services and nearly 30 anthems, two of which, *God which as at this time* and *Out of the deep*[2] are available in modern editions. Barnard printed his First Service and one anthem, *O give thanks*.

JOHN HILTON (d. 1608) is first heard of as a lay-clerk at Lincoln Cathedral in 1584. In 1594 he became organist of Trinity College, Cambridge. The anthem, *Lord, for thy tender mercy's sake*,[3] commonly attributed to him, is a perfect setting of a penitent's prayer. His seven-part *Call to remembrance*[4] is an excellent essay in contrapuntal writing. He was also one of the contributors to *The Triumphes of Oriana*.

JOHN HOLMES was organist of Winchester Cathedral and master of the choristers at Salisbury from 1621 till his death in 1629. Most of his church music survives in the 'Batten' organ book, including an evening service 'in medio chori', two settings of *Kyrie* and *Credo* 'to the organs', and *Preces* and psalms. It is naturally impossible to form an opinion of it from an organ part.

EDMUND HOOPER (1553–1621) was a very popular composer in his own day. His anthem *Behold it is Christ*, a strikingly original work, is found in almost all the seventeenth-century manuscript collections. Five services[5] and about 20 anthems,[6] three of which were printed by Barnard, represent his known output. He was Master of the Choristers at Westminster Abbey and one of the organists of the Chapel Royal.

THOMAS HUNT was one of the contributors to *The Triumphes of Oriana*. He is stated in the Barnard manuscript[7] to have been

---

[1] Jacob Rathgeb, *Kurtze und wahrhaffte Beschreibung der Badenfahrt* (1592), p. 17.

[2] Both ed. D. Keeling & B. Runnett (Oxford University Press).

[3] *Church Music Society*, No. 26.

[4] *Tudor Church Music*, 8vo ed., No. 97.

[5] Evening Services: Full Service, ed. P. le Huray (Oxford University Press); Verse Service, ed. P. le Huray (Oxford University Press).

[6] *Behold, it is Christ*, ed. P. le Huray (Schott); *Teach me thy way, O Lord*, *Church Music Society*, No. 21a.

[7] Royal College of Music, MS. 1051.

organist of Wells Cathedral. His short Morning and Evening Service of four parts is a useful little work characterized by some rather unusual harmonization.[1] Attached to this service is a setting of the *Preces and Responses*. Two or three of his anthems survive in manuscript.

MATTHEW JEFFREYS was another musician who, as a vicar-choral, was connected with Wells Cathedral early in the seventeenth century. Anthony Wood referred to him as an eminent musician. Two services and several anthems by this composer survive in manuscript.

GEORGE KIRBYE (*c.* 1565–1634) is best known as a madrigal-composer. He was resident musician for many years in the establishment of Sir Robert Jermyn at Rushbrooke Hall, near Bury St Edmunds. His career was very similar to that of Wilbye, who was his near neighbour at Hengrave Hall. He wrote little church music. The anthem *O Jesu, look*[2] is madrigalian in style and of much beauty, but the quaintness of the words rules it out of ordinary use in a church service.

HENRY and WILLIAM LAWES will be discussed in the next chapter.

SIR WILLIAM LEIGHTON (d. 1616) was one of the Gentlemen Pensioners at the Court of Elizabeth I and James I. He made a large collection of metrical psalms and hymns which were set to music by many of the most notable composers of the day. This was published in 1614 under the title *Teares or Lamentacions of a Sorrowful Soule* and was clearly intended for domestic use. Leighton himself wrote eight of the compositions: they are not distinguished by any special merit.

JOHN MUNDY (d. 1630) was the elder of two sons of William Mundy (see p. 59). As the family pedigree shows,[3] he was born about the year 1554. He succeeded Richard Farrant as one of the organists of St George's Chapel, Windsor, about 1580, and held this position till his death. In 1594 he published his *Songs and Psalmes composed into 3, 4 and 5 parts*. Half of these are sacred and half secular. A number of anthems (some

---

[1] *Tudor Church Music*, 8vo ed., Nos. 65 and 66.
[2] *Tudor Church Music*, 8vo ed., No. 18.
[3] British Museum, Harl. 5580, fo. 20.

incomplete) survive in manuscript; he also wrote some Latin motets. There is no particular distinction about the greater number of these, and his work is not on the same high level as his father's. It would seem that Barnard was also of this opinion, for whereas he included in his *Book of Selected Church Musick* a service and three anthems by the father, the son is represented by one anthem only. *Sing joyfully*,[1] however, is a fine verse anthem, with a vigorous baritone solo alternating with sections for full choir throughout the whole work. The declamatory passages for the solo voice show a keen appreciation of verbal accentuation. The accompaniment is written for strings; it shows a marked advance in the technique of the instruments, and is as good as anything of the kind in Gibbons's work. John Mundy wrote as many as nine services, including two evening services 'in medio chori' and two services 'for men', one in three parts, and one in four.

NATHANIEL PATTRICK was appointed master of the choristers at Worcester Cathedral in 1590, but died five years later. His Service in G minor[2] is sung in many cathedrals at the present time. It was not included in the collections of Barnard or Boyce, but Arnold printed it in his *Cathedral Music* (1790), assigning it incorrectly to Richard Pattrick, a lay-clerk of Westminster Abbey *c.* 1616.

FRANCIS PILKINGTON (d. 1638) was a minor canon and precentor of Chester Cathedral. In later years he was vicar of various churches in Chester. He devoted his gifts almost entirely to secular work. His two books of madrigals were issued in 1613 and 1624 respectively. His book of *Songs of Ayres* was an earlier work, published in 1605. He contributed two small sacred pieces to Leighton's *Teares or Lamentacions*. Two fine anthems are included in his second set of madrigals.[3] The six-part setting of Psalm 117, *O praise the Lord*, which follows next after his lovely madrigal *O softly-singing lute*, is finely written; the key-successions and general harmonization, involving several typical clashes between major and minor thirds, are worth

---

[1] *Tudor Church Music*, 8vo ed., No. 92.
[2] Ed. I. Atkins (Oxford University Press).
[3] *The English Madrigalists*, xxvi.

noting. The setting of the words 'for his merciful kindness' may
serve as an example:

The other anthem in this set is *O gracious God,* which is penitential in character.

WALTER PORTER (d. 1659) began his volume of *Madrigals
and Ayres,* published in 1632, with an anthem *O praise the Lord.*[1]

[1] *In the Treasury of English Church Music, 1540–1650,* ed. P. le Huray (Blandford
Press).

He was a pupil of Monteverdi, from whom he borrowed the device of rapidly repeated notes (a kind of *vibrato*), which, as he explained in his preface, were 'set to expresse the *Trillo*'. The following excerpt from this anthem will serve as an example:

He was master of the choristers at Westminster Abbey from 1639 to 1644.

RICHARD PORTMAN (d. 1656) was a pupil of Orlando Gibbons, and like him, became organist of Westminster Abbey. Of his three services, that in G major alone survives with complete text; and only one or two out of about a dozen anthems can be scored, for lack of sufficient text.

ROBERT RAMSEY[1] was appointed organist of Trinity College, Cambridge, in 1628. His Service in F major is a good example of the kind that so many of the lesser composers produced at this period. His six full anthems are a little stiff. The verse anthem *My song shall be alway* shows a greater freedom and an eye for effective declamation in a more up-to-date style:

[1] Complete English sacred music in *Early English Church Music*, vii.

My song, my song shall be al - way, shall be al - way of the loving kindness of the Lord, of the loving kindness of the Lord:

THOMAS RAVENSCROFT (*c.* 1590–*c.* 1633) wrote very little original church music; and his few anthems are of small consequence in relation to the work of his contemporaries. His edition of *The Whole Booke of Psalmes*, however, is an important publication. It was issued in 1621 and contains over 100 settings. All the musicians who contributed to East's Psalter are again represented here, and among new names are those of Thomas and John Hopkins, William Cranford, John Ward and John Milton, father of the poet.

NICHOLAS STROGERS, who flourished in the reign of James I, wrote three full services, as well as a Short Service which was printed by Barnard. Three anthems survive in manuscript.

JOHN WARD (1571–1638) was a madrigal-composer who also

wrote many fantasies for viols which are among the most interesting of the early examples of chamber music. His compositions for the Church are of less importance, though Barnard
thought well enough of them to include his First Evening
Service[1] and two verse anthems. Two more services and fifteen
more anthems[2] are to be found in manuscript and in Leighton's
collection. *Let God arise*, printed in Barnard's collection, is a
particularly fine work.

LEONARD WOODESON was a member of a Winchester family
of musicians. He became organist of Eton College in 1615. As
many as nine of his anthems as well as a morning service are
in the 'Batten' organ book, and a *Te Deum* was included by
Barnard in his *Selected Church Musick*.

JOHN BARNARD, a minor canon of St Paul's Cathedral, was
not a composer, but he did a work of incalculable value in
collecting the text of a large number of the best compositions of
the Elizabethan and Jacobean church musicians. His *First
Book of Selected Church Musick* was published in 1641. He made
a further collection which remains in manuscript.[3] These two
collections together have preserved the text of many services
and anthems which might otherwise have perished; the value of
his printed collection must also have been of great practical
use at the time of publication. Two years later cathedral music
was entirely suspended. No doubt a large number of copies of
Barnard's work perished in the period of the Commonwealth,
and this may account for the great rarity of complete sets of the
part-books today. But the work must have been immensely
useful to the cathedral musicians of the Restoration period,
when much of the Tudor music continued in use side by side
with the compositions of the new school. Evidence on this last
point is provided by the large number of manuscript part-books
made by cathedral copyists in the last quarter of the seventeenth century, notably at Durham.

Without detracting from the great practical usefulness of the
chief printed collections of the sixteenth, seventeenth and

---

[1] Ed. D. Wulstan (Oxford University Press).

[2] *O let me tread*, Church Music Society, No. 20; *O Lord, consider*, ed. J. F. Bridge
(Novello).

[3] Royal College of Music, MSS. 1045–51.

eighteenth centuries, there is an impoitant reservation to be made. Admittedly, as Barnard stated in the title-page of his printed collection, 'such Bookes as were heretofore with much difficulty and charges, transcribed for the use of the Quire, are now to the saving of much labour and expence, publisht for the general good of all such as shall desire them either for publick or private exercise'. When music-books for a choir are made available in such convenient form (and incidentally, printed music is easier than manuscript to sing from), it is inevitable that the choice of music for performance will be largely limited to what the printed books contain. In the light of modern knowledge it becomes apparent that Barnard had of necessity to omit a vast amount of beautiful works, many of which have only in the present century found their way back into use. Moreover the selection was based upon the taste of a single individual. The same reservation must be made in reference to Boyce's *Cathedral Music* in the eighteenth century. By that time the selection had to be made from an immensely larger field; and if Barnard had had to omit much, Boyce had to discard much that Barnard had been able to retain. The neglect of sixteenth- and early seventeenth-century church music in the nineteenth century may partly be explained in this way.

CHAPTER 10

Early Restoration Composers

The difficulty of classifying composers in groups, either by date or by the general character and features of their style, is nowhere more apparent than when dealing with the church musicians who were at work in the first few years after the Restoration of Charles II to the throne in 1660. It has been the common practice to employ the term the 'Restoration School of composers' to denote the period from 1660 until about the second decade of the eighteenth century, with Henry Purcell and John Blow as its conspicuous representatives.

It was not until Pelham Humfrey returned from Paris in 1667 that the full force of Italian and French influence had its effect upon English musicians. At that time Blow was only 19 years old and Purcell was 8. Humfrey himself was 20; Wise, Tudway and Turner were just a little younger. These six are the leading figures in a group which once more enabled English music to reach a position of eminence.

It is necessary, therefore, to consider the early Restoration composers as a separate group. Here the difficulties both of date and style are at once confronted, because they necessarily overlap. For example, William Child was born in 1606 and lived until 1697; he seems to have continued to compose throughout his long life and to have adhered almost entirely to the style of the older polyphonic school. Again, William Lawes was born in 1602 and died in 1645, so that he could not possibly be classified as a Restoration composer if dates alone were to be the measure of qualifications. Yet his anthem *The Lord is my light* is remarkable as an anticipation of the later Restoration composers in the matter of style and structure. For this reason he is included in the present chapter in spite of an apparent inconsistency.

The later years of the reign of Charles I had seen the growth of a new style of church music. It was essentially a period of transition. The leading feature of the newer developments was the increased use of the solo voice, both singly and in trios or quartets, as a contrast to the full choir of voices. At first the contrasted passages were limited to a single section of the composition. In course of time entire sections or movements came to be assigned to a solo voice alternating with sections for the full choir. Thus the structure of the work was enlarged, so that ultimately the form of the anthem took shape as a miniature cantata. The full development is seen in Purcell's more extended works. By the eighteenth century it had become the recognized classical design for the cathedral anthem. It was the form accepted and used by Boyce, and in the nineteenth century by S. S. Wesley.

Strangely enough the form of the service did not share in the developments shown in the design of the anthem. Indeed, the progressive ideas so conspicuously shown in the services of Morley, Weelkes, Tomkins and Gibbons were almost entirely absent from those by a composer such as Benjamin Rogers, who at this period reverted to the simple form of the Short Service and the note-against-note scheme in block harmony. Among the many services by Child there are some in which verse passages are introduced, but they all follow the Short Service form in principle, and can be sung without accompaniment.

A feature of some of the later Elizabethan and Jacobean services had been the employment of independent organ passages, not only for the accompaniment of the solo voice, but also as short interludes, especially in the opening bars. This feature also disappeared in the Restoration period. It is true that in Purcell's Service in B♭ major there are a large number of verses for trio and quartet, and also passages in imitative counterpoint; but there is no independent organ accompaniment, nor is the solo voice employed singly.

This retrogressive movement in the design of the service was probably due to the Puritan influence so strongly in evidence in connexion with the Prayer Book of 1662. What might be regarded as permissible in an anthem in the way of solo song or organ interlude was presumably to be strictly excluded from the musical performance of any of the canticles. This influence might also explain the discontinuance, and ultimately the total oblivion, of the verse services of the Elizabethans. The Short Services of Tallis, Byrd, Farrant and Gibbons did indeed survive in cathedral lists, but they owed their survival to the fact that they did not conflict, as the verse services did, with the restrained conventions of the two centuries that followed the period of the Commonwealth.

HENRY LAWES (1596–1662) was a gentleman of the Chapel Royal in Charles I's reign but was chiefly concerned with writing music for masques and secular songs. Milton's lines in his praise are frequently quoted; but Milton must have completely misunderstood the rhythmic features and subtle verbal accentuation of the Elizabethans if he sincerely believed that it was

> *Harry*, whose tunefull and well measur'd song
> First taught our English Music how to span
> Words with just note and accent.

In addition to Latin motets Lawes also wrote as many as 20 English anthems, of which all but six are incomplete or known only from the words. His anthem *Zadok the Priest*, composed for the coronation of Charles II, shows an understanding of the simple solemnity appropriate to a public occasion in a large building. It was sung again at James II's coronation.

WILLIAM LAWES (1602–45), brother of Henry, was a singer in the service of Charles I from 1635 and, like Henry, was chiefly concerned with secular music, particularly instrumental chamber works. In the Civil War he joined the Royalist army and was killed at the siege of Chester. His anthem *The Lord is my light*, printed by Boyce, is a work of some importance, being written in a style that would more readily suggest the authorship of one of the later Restoration composers. The detached use of several different solo voices in succession, as in the opening of this anthem,[1] is characteristic of the work of Michael Wise, for example, half a century later:

---

[1]British Museum, Add. 30,382, fo. 90ᵛ.

The trio with organ accompaniment is followed by a short chorus repeating the words 'And set me up upon a rock of stone':

Then follows a long quartet with contrapuntal imitations; and in the concluding chorus the final words of the quartet are repeated to fresh melodic material. This anthem has no great artistic value, but its historical importance is considerable. Three other anthems are known from manuscripts of the Restoration period.

WILLIAM CHILD (1606–97) was born shortly after the death of Elizabeth I and lived till within a few years of the accession of Queen Anne. For 67 years he lived at Windsor. Having been appointed an alto lay-clerk in 1630, he became organist and master of the choristers of St George's Chapel two years later. At Windsor he was within fairly easy distance from London, where he habitually carried out his duties as organist of the Chapel Royal, a post which he held simultaneously with that at Windsor.

His musical activities fall into two periods. He had already been at Windsor some thirteen years before the Chapel was closed during the period of the Civil War and the Commonwealth. His experience must have been a narrowing one, and his music gives evidence of a very conservative outlook on life. On his return to his duties at Windsor at the Restoration his activities seem to have had a rather wider scope. He became the close friend of Samuel Pepys, who made frequent mention of him in his *Diary*. There is the well-known entry[1] describing Pepys's visit to Windsor, where he 'sent for Dr. Childe; who come to us, and carried us to St. George's Chappell; and there placed us among the Knights' stalls'. Child was often at Lord Sandwich's house, introduced, as may be supposed, by the diarist. Thus on 21 December 1663: 'To my Lord Sandwich's, where I find him within with Captain Cooke and his boys, Dr. Childe, Mr. Madge, and Mallard, playing and singing over my Lord's anthem.' Child, truth to tell, was overmuch in London at this time in the opinion of the Dean and Chapter of Windsor, who admonished him to 'give assurance for better attendance in his office'.[2] In 1663 he took the D.Mus. degree at Oxford.

As a musician Child was by no means in the front rank. Very little of the large quantity of cathedral music which he wrote in his long life[3] survives in use today. Much of his work follows the old polyphonic methods. He looked more to the past than to the future, though he wrote a number of verse anthems and showed sympathy with Italian methods of declamation and harmonic treatment. Possibly he viewed the later Restoration

[1] 26 February 1666..

[2] Windsor Records, Chapter Minutes, 1 September 1662.

[3] For lists of his 17 Services and 62 anthems see P. le Huray, *Music and the Reformation in England, 1549–1660*, pp. 358–60.

composers, such as Humfrey, Blow and Purcell, without much sympathy, especially with reference to the introduction of symphonies and *ritornelli* for strings in their anthems. In any case he wrote nothing of the kind himself, as far as is known. He was over 70 years old when Purcell grew up, so it is scarcely surprising that he should not have been in sympathy with the new ideas.

His pre-Restoration Service in D major (he wrote nearly 20 in all), known at the time as his 'sharp' service, was very popular. It was said to have been a favourite with Charles II. Burney[1] admired this work, which he called Child's 'celebrated Service in D sharp', adding that it 'is extremely pleasing, the more so, perhaps from being composed in a key which is more perfectly in tune than most others on the organ'. Today it has a rather faded air.

The best of Child's full anthems that are generally accessible is *Sing we merrily*.[2] This was written as part of his exercise for the B.Mus. degree at Oxford in 1639. It is in eight parts, though the two tenor parts are seldom employed independently. This discloses an apparent defect in the part-writing, and it suggests that Child was at a loss in finding material to supply an eighth part, although he no doubt wanted the work to have the appearance of an eight-part motet as being more symmetrical and impressive, especially for a degree exercise. His own text of this anthem, scored on eight staves, is in manuscript at Windsor. The following passage will show the run of the two tenor parts, where the other six voices are fully treated with independent points of imitation. It is no more than an attempt to give a single part the appearance of two:

---

[1] *A General History of Music*, ii, p. 364.
[2] Ed. H. G. Ley (Novello).

The following passage from the verse anthem *Turn thou us, O good Lord*[1] will serve to illustrate Child's adaptation of Italian monody to English words:

BENJAMIN ROGERS (1614–98) was almost an exact contemporary of Child, and, like him, he lived to an advanced age. His father was a lay-clerk of St George's Chapel, Windsor, where he himself became a chorister. He had a somewhat chequered career. Before the Civil War he was organist of Christ Church Cathedral, Dublin. In 1662 he was appointed a lay-clerk at Windsor and acted as deputy organist to William Child, who at that time was much in London as organist of the Chapel Royal at Whitehall. For a time he was also organist of Eton College; and ultimately, in 1664, he became organist of Magdalen College, Oxford. This position he retained until 1685, when, owing to some disagreement with the college authorities, he retired on a pension. He was admitted to the Mus.B. degree at Cambridge in 1658 under a warrant from Cromwell[2] – which at least serves to illustrate the Protector's

---

[1] Ed. P. le Huray (Oxford University Press).
[2] P. A. Scholes, *The Puritans and Music in England and New England* (1934), pp. 137–8.

interest in music. His exercise for the D.Mus. degree at Oxford in 1669 was performed in the Sheldonian Theatre three days after the building was opened. It was thus the first of the long list of doctoral exercises officially performed there until the obligation was discontinued in 1889.

Like Child, Rogers was a conservative musician but composed far less. His Service in D major, for four voices, reverts to the older tradition of a single note to a syllable. But, unlike the Elizabethans, he keeps to a rhythm of four regular beats with little variation, and there are few contrapuntal features of imitation. In the *Credo* a little variety is introduced by some verse passages for three voices. This service is typical of many that followed it; it includes *Te Deum, Jubilate, Kyrie, Credo, Sanctus, Magnificat* and *Nunc dimittis*. Although *Jubilate* was seldom set by the Elizabethans, it was almost always preferred to *Benedictus* from the Restoration period onwards. Among Rogers's other services are those in A minor,[1] F major[2] and E minor.[1]

The type of Short Service established by Rogers formed the model followed by many of the eighteenth-century composers. But his services have a certain quality that is singularly lacking in the work of his eighteenth-century successors, such as, for example, Kent, Nares and Ebdon, whose music was so generally retained in use throughout the nineteenth century. It is perhaps the melodic interest, somewhat slender though it is, that still enables these services of Rogers to find favour with a few cathedral musicians who may have had associations with them as choristers. A new feature at this period, found also in Child's settings, was the substitution of a simple phrase of tonic and dominant in the place of the traditional plainsong intonations with which *Te Deum* had been formerly precented. The traditional intonations ought invariably to be used with the Elizabethan settings of *Te Deum* rather than this debased phrase invented in the early Restoration period.

Several short anthems by Rogers survive in use, though his longer ones are seldom heard. Three that are likely to keep his

---

[1] (Novello).
[2] Ed. C. F. Simkins (Banks).

name alive are *Lord, who shall dwell?*,[1] *Teach me, O Lord*[2] and
Behold now, praise the Lord.[3] The last two are especially suitable
for weekday morning services. *Behold now, praise the Lord* is spoilt
by a weakly homophonic setting of the word *Hallelujah*:

Child and Rogers were among the first to introduce this convention with which so many of the Restoration anthems end.
Even in the hands of Purcell and Blow the concluding *Halle-
lujahs* are sometimes trivial, although these composers occasionally succeeded in treating them with considerable interest and
purpose.

CHRISTOPHER GIBBONS (1615–76), son of Orlando, wrote
little church music, and even in the eighteenth century, according to Burney,[4] his compositions had 'long ceased to be performed in our cathedrals'. He was appointed organist of
Westminster Abbey at the time of the Restoration. He was

---

[1] Ed. C. F. Simkins (Hintichsen).
[2] Ed. A. Payson (Chappell).
[3] (Novello).
[4] *A General History of Music*, iii, p. 461.

succeeded there by Albert Bryan (or Bryne) who had been
organist of St Paul's Cathedral before the Civil War. A dull
service by Bryan[1] retained a place in some cathedral lists until
the end of the nineteenth century.

By far the most important musician belonging to the earlier
period of the Restoration is MATTHEW LOCKE (1622–77). Like
so many English musicians of note he began his career as a
cathedral chorister, in his native city Exeter. His reputation rests
mainly upon his work in the field of instrumental and dramatic
music. His treatise *Melothesia* (1673) is the earliest-known English work on the art of playing from a figured bass.[2] During the
period of the Commonwealth he showed great activity in composing music for strings and collaborated with Christopher
Gibbons in writing music for Shirley's masque *Cupid and Death*.
His church music was necessarily of a later date. On the return
of Charles II he was appointed composer-in-ordinary to the
king and organist to Queen Catherine. Several of his anthems
were written for the Chapel Royal. *Lord, let me know mine end*[3]
is designed on the extended scale that reached its full development in the hands of Humfrey, Blow and Purcell. Locke supplies
a kind of link between William Lawes and these three. The
anthem opens with a tenor solo, which may be quoted here as
showing a certain degree of stiffness in declamation:

---

[1] (Novello).

[2] See F. T. Arnold, *The Art of Accompaniment from a Figured Bass* (1931), p. 154.

[3] Ed. E. J. Dent & C. B. Rootham (Ascherberg Hopwood & Crew); also in *The Treasury of English Church Music, 1650–1760*, ed. C. Dearnley (Blandford Press).

The interval of the diminished fourth, used here as in Child's *Turn thou us, O good Lord,* was one of the hall-marks of the pathetic style which seventeenth-century English composers borrowed from the Italians. The diminished fifth, examples of which will be found in the excerpts from Humfrey's *By the waters of Babylon* (quoted on pp. 137–8), served a similar purpose.

After the passage quoted above there follows a trio, and a short chorus 'And verily every man living'. The rest of the anthem is laid out in sections with solo work and chorus alternating. The final chorus 'O spare me a little' follows a quartet of solo voices written to the same words.

Locke's anthems for men's voices can be useful today on occasions when boys are not available, but they are not particularly distinguished. He set no service to music, as far as is known, except a *Kyrie* and *Credo* in which he wrote different music for each response to the Commandments. This feature seems to have met with active resentment by the Chapel Royal choir. Their attitude may partly be accounted for by the fact that Locke was not an easy man to get on with.

WILLIAM KING (1624–80) calls for passing mention as having composed a Litany which is still sometimes to be heard, though it is very inferior to the sixteenth-century settings. It is constructed without any reference to the traditional plainsong. King became organist of New College, Oxford, in 1664. He wrote some anthems and a service.

HENRY LOOSEMORE (d. 1670), who was organist of King's College, Cambridge, from 1627, wrote two settings of the Litany, one of which is still sung sometimes; but the treatment of the plainsong melody in the minor key is out of keeping with all ancient tradition. More important are his 30 anthems, of which 19 were written before the Commonwealth. Many of them have survived incomplete; but the accident of erroneous attribution to Orlando Gibbons has made familiar the full anthems *O Lord, increase our faith* and *Why art thou so heavy?*[1]

[1] *Tudor Church Music*, iv, pp. 270 and 315.

The Restoration Period — I

Humfrey and Blow

The Restoration period is the most picturesque in the history of English church music. It centres round the activities of the Chapel Royal at Whitehall. It is not fully realized how circumscribed was the scope of these activities, carried on as they were with such large results almost entirely within the narrow limits of the Chapel itself. The Chapel Royal musicians were producing new works, many of them of the highest artistic value, at the rate of one a month and sometimes even more rapidly. The text of a very large proportion of these compositions survives today; consequently the impression prevails that the movement was a national one. It remains a fact, however, that several years elapsed before the influence of this London group spread to the provincial cathedrals and collegiate churches. When the term 'Restoration music' is used now in relation to church music, it means in practice the music of three particular composers: Pelham Humfrey, John Blow and Henry Purcell, of whom Purcell was the greatest. Lesser men belonging to this group were Thomas Tudway, William Turner and Michael Wise. Of these Tudway was a self-confessed conservative in musical matters,[1] and his influence at Cambridge, where he became Professor of Music, was definitely opposed to the new type of anthem, even though he came under the Italian influence like the rest. Turner, except for a very short time at Lincoln, was a Londoner. Wise, it is true, was living in the provinces as organist of Salisbury in and after 1668, but he must have spent much of his time in London after 1675, when he was appointed

---

[1] British Museum, Harl. 7338, preface.

a countertenor in the Chapel Royal. It is unlikely that the new influence reached Salisbury until after his time.

The story begins with HENRY COOKE (d. 1672). He was a picturesque personality. Born late in the reign of James I, the son, as is thought, of a cathedral singer at Lichfield and the Chapel Royal, he began his musical career as one of the Children of the Chapel. The Civil War broke out soon after he had grown to manhood. He joined the army in support of the king and rose to the rank of captain. During the Commonwealth it seems that he spent some time in Italy. If so, this would be in keeping with the Italian influence that is characteristic of the work of his pupils.

At the Restoration he was appointed to the Chapel Royal as a bass singer and master of the children. As a singer he earned a great reputation. He was frequently praised by Samuel Pepys, who noted that 'without doubt he hath the best manner of singing in the world'.[1] Pepys also once called him 'a vain coxcomb' and added that 'his bragging . . . I do not like by no means'.[2] That may have been in a moment of irritation, but Cooke certainly had his head turned by his success as a singer. On another occasion Pepys commented on an anthem at the Chapel Royal and added: 'But yet I could discern Captain Cooke to overdo his part at singing, which I never did before.'[3] However, it was as a trainer of boy singers that Cooke earned undying fame.

As an old Chapel Royal boy himself, he knew what to aim at. The task was a formidable one. Men singers presented no great difficulty, for the interval of seventeen years had not left the field quite empty, as it had in the case of choristers. At first he was compelled to supplement the boys' voices with the treble cornett, which had a compass closely corresponding to that of a boy's voice. It was an emergency measure, soon to give place to a remarkable set of boy choristers. Cooke achieved this feat of organization by reviving the warrant under which he was empowered to conscript boys with good voices from the choirs of any cathedral or church and bring them to Whitehall. He once overreached his powers when, with the apparent

<hr>

[1] 27 July 1661.   [2] 13 February 1667.   [3] 14 September 1662.

connivance of Child, he conscripted two of the boys from St
George's Chapel. The Windsor Chapter, as a minute dated 22
April 1664 shows, appealed successfully to the Lord Chancellor
to protect them from 'the insolencys of Mr. Cooke (Mr of the
King's boys) committed lately against this Free Chappell in
his stealing away two of our Choristers without any special
warrant contrary to the priviledge of this place'. But Cooke
certainly showed unusual acumen in securing, among others,
Pelham Humfrey, John Blow, Michael Wise, Thomas Tudway
and William Turner. A little later Henry Purcell was to
become one of the children, but he was younger than these five.
Humfrey, Blow and Wise were about 12 or 13 at the time,
while Turner and Tudway were two or three years younger.
An early mention of Cooke's boys is recorded by Pepys on 23
February 1661: 'To Whitehall Chappell with Mr. Child and
there did hear Captain Cooke and his boy [sic] make a trial of
an Anthem against to-morrow, which was brave musique.'

Cooke himself played a large part in providing the Sunday
anthems at the Chapel Royal, both as a singer and as a composer. His compositions are not of much merit, though Pepys
wrote on 12 August 1660: 'After sermon a brave anthem of
Captain Cooke's, which he himself sung, and the King was
well pleased with it.' It is clear that the new design of anthem
was already establishing itself; declamatory solos, and even
short organ *ritornelli*, were being introduced in the very first
months of the Restoration, as a natural development of musical
taste which was already foreshadowed in England, both in
secular and sacred music, before the Civil War. The design of
William Lawes's verse anthem has already been mentioned.
At the same time the old polyphonic anthems still occupied a
fair share of the repertory, even in the Chapel Royal.

Tudway attributed the introduction of the new style to
Charles II's individual taste. No doubt he was right in saying
that the king was responsible for introducing a string band into
the Chapel and for ordering symphonies and *ritornelli* to be
performed between the verses of the anthems on Sundays and
festivals. But that the verse anthem would have developed on
the lines already foreshadowed is a certainty, quite apart from

any royal instructions, at a time when such composers as Purcell, Humfrey and Blow were exercising their great gifts. Charles II took a keen interest in the choir of the Chapel Royal, and at his own expense increased the number of the singers. He did not order the complete exclusion of polyphonic music, but he realized that the new style of verse anthem might be greatly improved if a string band were provided and symphonies and *ritornelli* introduced on the plan that had become familiar to him in France. Accordingly the twenty-four violins,[1] established on the model of Louis XIV's 'Vingt-quatre violons du roi', were given the additional duty of taking part in services in the Chapel Royal.

It was on Sunday, 14 September 1662, according to Pepys, that the string instruments were first heard in the new type of anthem. He wrote: 'This first day of having vialls[2] and other instruments to play a symphony between every verse of the anthem.' Two months later Evelyn noted in his diary:[3] 'Instead of the antient grave and solemn wind musique accompanying the organ, was introduced a Consort of 24 Violins betweene every pause, after the *French* fantastical light way, better suiting a Tavern or Play-house than a Church. This was the first time of change, and now we no more heard the cornet which gave life to the organ, that instrument quite left off in which the English were so skilful.' The innovation probably provoked a good deal of controversy at the time even among musicians. Many years later, in 1716, Tudway recorded his opinion about it in plain terms in the long preface which he addressed to Lord Harley in the second volume of his manuscript collection of church music.[4] The opinion is curious in view of the fact that he was one of Cooke's choristers and wrote some anthems of this kind himself. He puts forward

the reason as I conceive, how we are fall'n into this Theatricall & Secular Style, in our Compositions of Church music. King Charles the 2[d] being restor'd to his Just Rights, and with him the Church of England to its Ancient use, & dissipline; The 1st

---

[1] i.e. violins, violas and cellos.
[2] Either Pepys was writing carelessly or 'vialls' is an error in transcription.
[3] 21 December 1662.   [4] British Museum, Harl. 7338.

thing thought of, was to settle the divine Service, & worship, in his Majestys Chappell Royall, after such a modell, as the Cathedralls . . .

The King took great delight in the Service of his Chappell, & was very intent upon Establishing his Choir, and had the goodness to make such an addition, as allmost to double[1] the number of Gentlemen, & Children of the Chappell which it consisted of before the Rebellion . . .

His Majesty who was a brisk, & Airy Prince, comeing to the Crown in the Flow'r, & vigour of his Age, was soon, if I may so say, tyr'd with the Grave & solemn way, And Order'd the Composers of his Chappell, to add symphonys &c with Instruments to their Anthems; and therupon Establis'd a select number of his private music, to play the symphonys, & Retornellos, which he had appointed . . .

In about 4 or 5 years time, some of the forwardest, & brightest Children of the Chappell, as Mr. Humfreys, Mr. Blow, &c began to be Masters of a faculty in Composing; This, his Majesty greatly encourag'd, by indulging their youthful fancys, so that ev'ry month at least, & afterwards oft'ner, they produc'd something New, of this Kind . . . Thus this secular way was first introduc'd into the service of the Chappell, And has been too much imitated ever since, by our modern Composers; After the death of King Charles, symphonys, indeed, with Instruments in the Chappell, were laid aside; But they continu'd to make their Anthems with all the Flourishes of interludes, & Retornellos, which are now perform'd by the Organ.

This however did not Oblige the Cathedrals throughout England, to follow such an Example; for indeed such an Example was very improper for their imitation; because they had none of the fine voices, which his Majesty had in his Chappell, to perform light solos . . . But the Composers of those, and later times, being Charm'd, with what they heard at White Hall, never consider'd how improper such Theatricall performances are, in religious Worship . . . [they] serve to create delight rather than to actuate devotion.

Tudway's reference to the exceptional excellence of the men's voices at Whitehall is significant. Among the basses was John Gostling, for whom Purcell and others wrote passages covering a very wide compass. But the altos must have been exceptionally good. Michael Wise was one who was evidently

---

[1] This is an exaggeration.

outstanding; William Child was another, and there were many more. The composers at the Chapel Royal had these singers in their minds when they wrote not only solos, but the numberless verses for men's voices with the altos at the top. Tudway was right; it is still a mistake to attempt to perform this music and much of that of the following century, unless adequate voices, especially altos, are available. A good balance of tone is only rarely secured in the verse passages in modern performances, and the effect is often made intolerable by a kind of false tradition that all passages of this sort must be taken at a slow tempo, and after a short pause following the previous movement.

As regards the introduction of instruments, it seems strange to modern musicians that they should have been considered by Tudway and others to be secular and theatrical; but it must be remembered that they were a complete novelty, upsetting all conservative ideas at the time. Moreover this was a period in which a large section of the community regarded even the organ as an instrument unsuited to religious worship. More significant than the use of instruments was the greatly increased employment of solo song. It had been foreshadowed long before by Gibbons. It took shape in the hands of Purcell and his contemporaries. It was further developed by Croft, Greene and Boyce in the eighteenth century, and it culminated in the arias of S. S. Wesley.

PELHAM HUMFREY (1647–74) was the eldest of Cooke's choristers. He left the choir in 1664 and was sent abroad by Charles II, who contributed £200 out of the Secret Service Fund for his travelling expenses in Italy and France; a further £250 was spread over the following two years. There is no definite evidence of his having studied with Lully, although it would seem probable that he came into contact with the musicians of the French Court, of whom Lully was chief, particularly as he had the recommendation of Charles II behind him. What he learned in Italy (if he ever got there) is uncertain; but in fact he could have acquired some knowledge of the Italian style from Cooke, who was described as a singer 'after the Italian manner' and taught his choristers to sing Italian songs.

In matters of dress and general deportment, no doubt Humfrey came under the spell of French fashion, so that on his return to Whitehall in 1667 Pepys, finding him at the tailor's, called him 'an absolute Monsieur'.[1] On Cooke's death in 1672 he succeeded him as master of the children. Meanwhile he had married Cooke's daughter. He died at the age of 27, when Henry Purcell was about 15.

Humfrey's church music is uneven in quality. That he could reach a very high level of excellence is shown in his anthem *By the waters of Babylon*, which bears comparison with the finest even of Purcell's works.[2] The declamatory passages are designed with much dramatic force and expression, without any of the extravagances that mar so much of the music of this period. The work begins with a short overture of nineteen bars in slow time, in a style that at once establishes the mood of homesick grief felt by the exiles in Babylon:

<hr>

[1] 15 November 1667.

[2] The statement of Philip Hayes, written by him on an early transcription of this anthem in Purcell's hand (British Museum, Add. 30,932), to the effect that Humfrey's work was 'much improv'd and enlarg'd by Purcell', is false.

The opening verse is given to a solo bass voice with violin obbligato:

The bullying Babylonians, with a short phrase in quick triple measure call to them: 'Sing us! – Sing us one of the songs of Sion!' The answer is given by a trio of two tenors and a bass:

The command to sing is repeated. The answer this time is expressed more harshly:

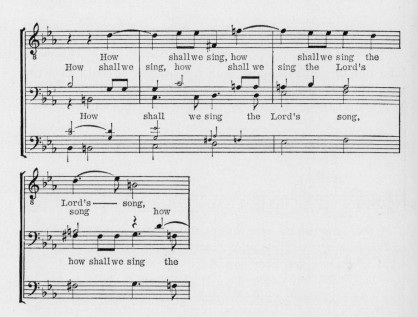

The anthem ends with a chorus beginning with imitative entries:

Humfrey favoured minor keys in his anthems. This not only
enabled him to write expressive declamation in the pathetic
style in which he excelled but also to introduce the singing with
instrumental movements of great dignity. The introduction to
By the waters of Babylon has already been quoted; here, for the
sake of comparison, is the opening of *O Lord my God*:[1]

[1] In *The Treasury of English Church Music, 1650–1760*, ed. C. Dearnley (Blandford
Press).

Not all the anthems have instrumental introductions, or indeed *ritornelli*. *Hear, O heavens*,[1] at any rate in the form in which it has come down to us, is with organ only, and there are no interludes. The opening of this anthem is a fine example of the power and pathos of Humfrey's declamation:

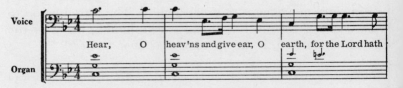

[1] Ed. W. Bowie (Oxford University Press).

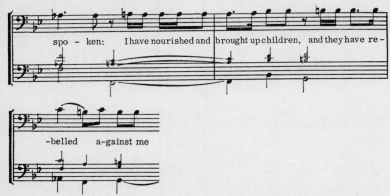

spo - ken: I have nourished and brought up children, and they have re -

-belled a-gainst me

Humfrey did not confine himself to alto, tenor and bass voices for the verse sections. Among the examples of solos for trebles is this invigorating verse from *Hear my crying, O God*:

Voice — From the ends of the earth will I call up-on thee,

Violin

Organ

from the ends of the earth will I call up-on

thee, when my heart is in hea - vi-ness, from the ends of the earth will I

JOHN BLOW (1649–178) was slightly younger than Humfrey, but he survived both him and Purcell by many years, and his compositions cover a comparatively long period in relation to the transitional character of music during his lifetime. He was nearly 12 years old when he became a chorister at the Chapel Royal under Cooke. In 1668, at the age of 19, he was appointed organist of Westminster Abbey in succession to Albert Bryan (or Bryne). On the death of Pelham Humfrey in 1674 he succeeded his old school-fellow as master of the children of the Chapel Royal. In 1677 he was awarded the Lambeth degree of D.Mus. – the earliest recipient, as far as is known. In 1679 he left his post at the Abbey and was succeeded by his pupil Henry Purcell, who was then about 20 years old. After Purcell's death in 1695 he came back as the Abbey organist and held the position until his death.

Blow was a voluminous composer. He wrote nearly 100 anthems as well as eleven Latin motets and eleven Services. His earliest anthems date from his chorister days, for the words of three of them were included in Clifford's *Divine Services and Anthems*, which was published in 1663.

Among the anthems with strings are two written for coronations: *God spake sometime in visions*, for the coronation of James II, and *The Lord God is a sun and shield*, for the coronation of William III and Mary. *God spake sometime in visions*[1] is a majestic and spacious work, clearly designed, like Purcell's *My heart is inditing*, to make full use of all the resources available. The voices required are two trebles, two altos, tenor and three basses,

---

[1] *Musica Britannica*, vii, pp. 1–45.

though they do not always have independent parts. Here Blow combines the older polyphonic tradition with more modern homophonic contrast between voices and instruments, as in the verse 'I will smite down his foes before his face':

Blow also wrote an anthem with strings, *I was glad when they said unto me*, for the opening of St Paul's Cathedral (1697). Among the other works of this kind (two of which include trumpets and one recorders and oboes) are *And I heard a great voice*[1] (known in the past from an adaptation beginning with the words 'I was in the spirit'), the suave and gracious *The Lord is my shepherd*,[2] and *I said in the cutting off of my days*.[3] The last of these is an impressive piece, especially in the latter sections. It begins with a four-bar introduction for strings, employing the same melodic material as in the tenor solo that follows. In declamation this solo falls below the standard reached by Humfrey and Purcell, and the verbal accentuation is not uniformly good. Various sections follow which include trios and quartets for men's voices, interspersed with *ritornelli*. The anthem ends with a brilliant 'Hallelujah', sung by the full chorus:

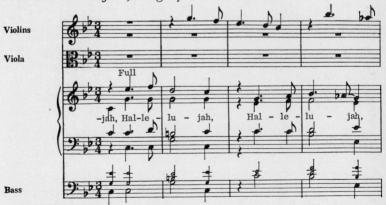

[1] *Musica Britannica*, pp. 62–77.
[2] *Ibid.*, pp. 93–108. Bliss's orchestral *Meditations on a theme by John Blow* are based on a melody in triple time in the overture to this anthem.
[3] *Ibid.*, pp. 78–91.

Hal - le - lu - jah, Hal - le - lu -

- jah.

A splendid example of Blow's work in the old polyphonic style is his *O Lord God of my salvation*,[1] written in massive eight-part counterpoint. The following passage, showing a free use of chromatic harmonies, comes at the very end of the anthem:

[1] Ed. H. Watkins Shaw,

Large-scale works of equally fine quality include *God is our hope and strength*,[1] for eight voices, *O God, wherefore art thou absent*[2] and *Sing we merrily*,[3] both for six voices. There are also a number of works for four voices which, in varying degrees, take their inspiration from the older polyphonic style. Several of these are penitential in character: they include *Be merciful unto me, O Lord*,[4] *Bow down thine ear*,[5] *My days are gone like a shadow*,[6] *My*

[1] Ed. H. Statham (Oxford University Press).
[2] Ed. J. E. West (Novello). [3] Ed. C. Macpherson (Novello).
[4] *Church Music Society*, No. 31.
[5] Ed. H. Statham (Oxford University Press).
[6] *Church Music Society*.

God, my God, look upon me,[1] and *Put me not to rebuke.*[2] The imitative opening of *My God, my God, look upon me,* repeated at the end of the anthem, is a powerful expression of despair. The opening of *Bow down thine ear* may serve as an example of this side of Blow's work:

[1] Ed. G. Bantock (Curwen).
[2] Ed. H. Statham (Oxford University Press).

Blow's services include three different settings in G major: in one of these[1] the *Gloria* of *Magnificat* is a three-fold canon for treble, alto and tenor:

The services in D minor[2] and F major[3] are straightforward pieces of work in four parts. The *Gloria* of *Nunc dimittis* in the F major service is curiously reminiscent, in its scale passages, of Gibbons's work in the same key. The D minor, or 'Dorian',

[1] Transposed to A major, ed. H. Watkins Shaw (Stainer & Bell).
[2] *Church Music Society*, No. 34.
[3] In *The Treasury of English Church Music, 1650–1760*, ed. C. Dearnley (Blandford Press).

Service, an excellent and singable work, is written somewhat in the style of the Elizabethan composers, introducing variety in the rhythmic treatment of the phrases. It also includes characteristic examples of Blow's harmony. The most interesting of the verse services is the setting in G major which Boyce included in his *Cathedral Music*. There is greater freedom in the part-writing than is found in the other services, and the verse sections form an effective contrast to those for the full choir. It includes all the alternative canticles, *Benedictus*, *Jubilate*, *Magnificat*, *Nunc dimittis*, *Cantate* and *Deus misereatur*. Blow also added a *Sanctus* and *Gloria in excelsis*; whether this was done with the idea of being comprehensive, or for the express purpose of providing music for the Communion Office in full, cannot be determined. It is noteworthy that he wrote another setting of *Sanctus* and *Gloria in excelsis* in the key of D major.

CHAPTER 12

The Restoration Period – II

Wise, Tudway and Turner

It seems right to consider next the work of the lesser Restoration composers, headed by the rest of Cooke's boys – Michael Wise, Thomas Tudway and William Turner – before passing to the subject of Henry Purcell's church music, which must call for a separate chapter.

MICHAEL WISE (d. 1687) was a better musician than either Tudway or Turner, though he produced far fewer compositions than they did. The date of his birth is not precisely known. It cannot well have been later than 1648; his name appears in the records of St George's Chapel, Windsor, as one of the signatories to a memorandum in 1666. He was probably born at Salisbury. He entered the Chapel Royal as a chorister under Cooke in 1660. In 1668 he became organist of Salisbury Cathedral; but he was frequently absent from his duties after being appointed a Gentleman of the Chapel Royal as a countertenor in 1676. Early in 1687 he became almoner and master of the choristers of St Paul's Cathedral. He met with a violent death at the hands of a watchman, according to Anthony Wood and others, but whether in London or Salisbury is uncertain. There is no record of his having been buried at Salisbury. As the Salisbury Cathedral records show, he was a man of a very difficult and quarrelsome disposition.[1]

He was not a prolific composer. Four of his anthems are well known today: *Awake, awake, put on thy strength*;[2] *Prepare ye the*

---

[1] D. H. Robertson, *Sarum Close*, pp. 201–4.
[2] (Novello).

way;[1] *The ways of Sion do mourn*;[2] and *Awake up, my glory*.[3] All these are unpretentious in scope and design, but they are distinguished by a strong feeling for melodic beauty and for structural form. For example, both in *Awake up, my glory* and in *The ways of Sion*, the repetition of short choral sections at intervals between the verse passages has the effect of binding together the separate sections into one whole. *The ways of Sion* is perhaps the best of these four. The treble and bass duets, it is true, are a little too long, and the combination of these voices, so far apart in compass and quality, is apt to sound thin; but the phrases are beautifully shaped and very expressive. The treble solo that follows the short chorus 'See, O Lord, and consider' is admirable in expression, and the repetition of the word 'nothing' adds much to the pathos of the appeal:

[1] (Novello).
[2] Ed. C. H. Kitson (Bayley & Ferguson); also in *The Treasury of English Church Music, 1650–1760*, ed. C. Dearnley (Blandford Press).
[3] Ed. B. Luard Selby (Stainer & Bell).

Thy beauty, O Israel[1] is an expressive treatment of David's lament for the death of Saul and Jonathan. Wise was less successful when aiming at more ambitious designs for his anthems. For example, in *O praise God in his holiness* the florid passages for the voices are conventional and uninspired: 'the sound of the trumpet' is represented by a verse which deserts the imitation of the trumpet in favour of an anticipation of the string *ritornello*:

I will sing a new song is a better example of an anthem with symphonies for strings. *Have pity upon me* was popular in Wise's own time, and so were *Blessed is he that considereth* and *By the waters of Babylon*, judging by their appearing in many manuscripts. These three are early works, for they are found in a manuscript dated 1669.[2]

[1] Ed. W. H. Harris, with Aldrich's additions (Novello).
[2] Tenbury MS. 1442.

Wise's Service in D minor comprises *Te Deum, Jubilate, Kyrie, Credo, Sanctus, Magnificat* and *Nunc dimittis*. His service in E♭ major includes only the evening canticles. It is an excellent example of the Short Service form as represented at this period, almost entirely in block harmony.

The music of THOMAS TUDWAY (*c*. 1650–1726) no longer holds a place in cathedral choirs, but he has some importance in the light of actual achievement, which must necessarily include the very valuable and laborious task of compiling for Lord Harley the six weighty volumes of services and anthems now in the British Museum.[1]

He was, no doubt, the son of Thomas Tudway, who was already a lay-clerk of St George's Chapel, Windsor, before 1664.[2] He was young enough *c*. 1660 to be appointed one of the Chapel Royal choristers. In 1670 he succeeded Henry Loosemore as organist of King's College, Cambridge, and in course of time proceeded to the degrees of Mus.B. and Mus.D. In 1705 he became Professor of Music in Cambridge University. At the age of about 65 he began to compile his collection of cathedral music, a task that occupied him for six years.

Tudway included 18 of his own anthems in his Harleian Collection. His views about the introduction of *ritornelli* and their theatrical effect have already been mentioned (see p. 133). Nevertheless he evidently found it impossible to hold out entirely against the popular demand for anthems of this character. His anthem *My heart rejoiceth*, which was written for the Thanksgiving Service after the Peace of Ryswick (1697), is very long and must be ranked as a short cantata, as will be seen from the following schedule of its various sections. It is not a work of great musical interest:

1. Instrumental overture: Adagio and Allegro.
2. Tenor solo: *My heart rejoiceth*.
3. Verse (alto and tenor): *There is none holy as the Lord*.
4. Verse (S.A.T.B.) with instrumental accompaniment: *The Lord liveth*.

[1] Harl. 7337–42.
[2] St George's Chapel Registers.

5. Verse (A.A.T.B.) and chorus *a cappella*: *Even the God that subdueth*.

6. Alto solo: *He hath delivered me*.

7. Verse (A.A.T.B.) and chorus with instrumental symphonies: *This is the Lord*.

8. Instrumental introduction and bass solo: *He maketh wars to cease*.

9. Verse (A.A.T.B.) and chorus with instruments: *O pray for the peace*.

10. Verse (A.A.T.B.) and chorus with instruments: *The Lord shall judge*.

Is it true that God will dwell is another of Tudway's anthems with symphonies between certain sections; but these are written for organ, not strings. This anthem was composed for the opening of St Paul's Cathedral in 1697. *I will lift up mine eyes* is written for a very extended tenor solo in a flamboyant style, including phrases in demisemiquavers. No more than a short conventional *Hallelujah* for chorus is added to this solo to complete the anthem. *Sing, O heavens* has an organ part with a direction 'trumpet stop'. There is a similar direction in the anthem *I will sing unto the Lord for he hath triumphed*, which was written for the Thanksgiving Service after the battle of Blenheim in 1704.

Tudway's verse Evening Service in B♭ major is written in a very elaborate style. The opening of *Magnificat* will illustrate the florid writing, not only for the solo voice but also for the organ:

WILLIAM TURNER (1651–1740), the third of this group of Cooke's choristers, was born in Oxford and began his career in the Christ Church choir. He passed on to the Chapel Royal, probably under Cooke's warrant empowering him to commandeer boys for the choir. Like Wise, he developed later a countertenor voice and went first as a lay-clerk to Lincoln

Cathedral. He came back to London as a Gentleman of the Chapel Royal in 1669. With several alto singers of this class at the Chapel, it is no wonder that the composers made liberal use of the alto voice both for solo work and also for trios of men's voices in the manner that became a regular convention at this period. The excellence of the men's voices must also be one of the explanations of the curious fact that solos for boys' voices did not come into vogue until a later generation. Before the closing years of the century composers, as far as is known, wrote very few treble solos in their anthems, or even passages for duet or trio in which a boy sang the upper part. The treble solo in Wise's anthem *The ways of Sion* is one of the early examples of the kind, and even in that instance the higher register of the voice is not brought into use. Purcell only very occasionally wrote solos for boys.

Turner lived to a great age. In the course of time he served as a lay-clerk at St Paul's Cathedral and also at Westminster Abbey. He took the Mus.D. degree at Cambridge in 1696. Both he and his wife were buried in Westminster Abbey. Though so many years of his life were spent in choir work, he did not compose much church music. He seems to have had a preference for writing songs and catches and other secular music. Two services and about sixteen anthems are all that is known of his church music. His earliest effort at composition was his share in the production of the 'Club' anthem, which was written jointly by Humfrey, Blow and Turner when they were still choristers.

By far the most important of his compositions is his anthem *The king shall rejoice*. This was written for performance on St Cecilia's Day 1697 in St Paul's Cathedral, the cathedral choir being augmented by the choirs of Westminster Abbey and the Chapel Royal. It is much longer than the ordinary anthem and is really a considerable cantata, like so many of Purcell's anthems with symphonies. The string band in this instance was supplemented by two trumpets. The overture begins with a characteristic phrase for the trumpets, answered in the dominant by the strings:

Though a little too ornate in places, this is a work of considerable interest and it might be worth performing in conditions
other than those of an ordinary cathedral service. The treble
solo is an early example of its kind in using the high register:

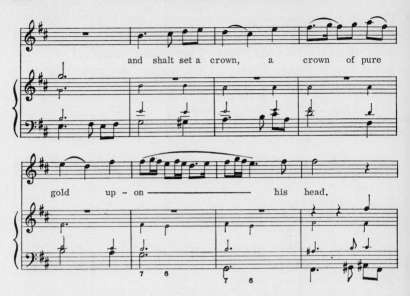

and shalt set a crown, a crown of pure

gold up - on ———————————— his head.

The final chorus 'So will we sing' is accompanied by trumpets and strings. A more intimate side of Turner's work may be illustrated by this excerpt from the anthem *Lord, thou hast been our refuge*,[1] which in spite of some awkward word-setting is genuinely expressive:

For a thou - sand years in thy sight are but as yes - ter -

day, see - ing that is past as a watch in the night, see -

[1] Ed. H. G. Ley (Banks).

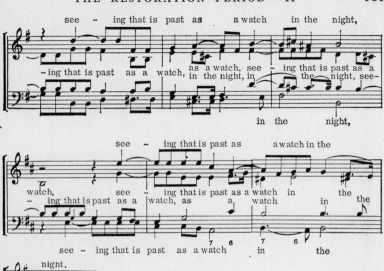

WILLIAM TUCKER (d. 1679) was older than the group of Chapel Royal boys, having been admitted as a gentleman of the Chapel at the time of the Restoration. He was ordained a little later and became a minor canon and precentor of Westminster Abbey. Among his anthems *O give thanks*[1] had a wide popularity that extended to the end of the nineteenth century. The choice of *Comfort ye, my people* as the subject of one of his anthems may conceivably have suggested these words to Charles Jennens, the librettist of Handel's *Messiah*. In addition to two services he also composed a *Benedicite*.

[1] (Novello).

CHAPTER 13

The Restoration Period – III:

Purcell

HENRY PURCELL (*c.* 1659–95), the most distinguished musician of his time, was the son of a gentleman of the Chapel Royal. He began his career as a chorister in the Chapel and left the choir when his voice broke in 1673. He had been a pupil of Humfrey, and he was soon to come under the instruction of Blow. Meanwhile he undertook an unsalaried appointment to look after the king's musical instruments, as assistant to John Hingston. This brought him into touch with the organ at Westminster Abbey, and at this period he received payment for doing some musical copying there. In 1677 he succeeded Matthew Locke as Composer for the King's Violins, a position offering valuable experience for him. It cannot be doubted that he would have been a practical violinist as well as an organist. At an earlier date the Windsor choristers were taught to play instruments as part of their routine, and the same practice prevailed at the Chapel Royal. In 1679, when Blow gave up the appointment, Purcell became organist of the Abbey and held this position until his death. In 1682 he became one of the three organists of the Chapel Royal, an appointment that included the duty, in his turn, of singing in the choir; it appears that, like many cathedral singers since his day, he could sing either bass or alto.

Purcell's great reputation as a composer has never stood higher than it does now; yet there exists a widespread opinion that his church music, with a few exceptions, does not reach the same outstanding excellence as his secular work. Parry deplored 'the extravagant extent to which Purcell's work of this kind differed from the old devotional Church music',[1] and in his own time there were those who regarded his anthems as theatrical and secular in character.

Purcell's anthems fall into three classes: (1) those written in the older style which can generally be sung effectively without accompaniment; (2) those written with an accompaniment for the organ; (3) those written with symphonies and *ritornelli* for strings. The third of these classes is far the most important: it includes numbers of compositions that rank among the best examples in this particular field. Yet there are good reasons why most of them are excluded from ordinary cathedral use. They lose much of their artistic effect if the organ is substituted for strings in the performance of the symphonies, especially as the string idiom is largely unsuited to the organ. They lose still more if ruthless cuts are made, either of the symphonies or the vocal sections. Yet, if performed in full, most of them are too long for daily Evensong. And lastly, exceptionally good men singers, especially altos, are indispensable. Of necessity their performance must be reserved for special occasions when they can be heard in the conditions for which the composer wrote them. Though it is true, as Parry remarked, that these anthems differed widely from Elizabethan works, 'extravagant' seems to be the wrong adjective to apply. They were the natural consequence of contemporary conditions.

The charge of theatricality and secularity must be seriously considered. Although viols had been used by Gibbons and Byrd for the accompaniment of their anthems, violins in church were a novelty. It is not surprising that these new and more brilliant-toned instruments were regarded by many as a secular intrusion, having hitherto been heard only in the theatre and the tavern. Violins even in secular surroundings were still something of a novelty, for although the violin had reached perfection in the hands of Andrea Amati as early as 1565, the best part of a century passed before the violin family entirely replaced that of the viols in England. Whether he was himself a violinist or not, Purcell undoubtedly fully understood violin technique – witness his *Sonnatas of III Parts*. The symphonies

[1] *Oxford History of Music*, iii, p. 278.

of his anthems are admirably suited to strings. Among the characteristic features are the successions of dotted quavers and semiquavers which recur so frequently.

The charge of theatricality is not entirely to be set aside. To say this is not to criticize the principles of word-painting which Purcell and his contemporaries inherited from the Elizabethans. Nothing for instance could be more charming and artistic than 'the singing of the birds' and 'the voice of the turtle' in *My beloved spake*:[1]

[1] *Purcell Society*, xiii.

but the temptation to write extravagant virtuoso passages for a famous singer was evidently too strong for Purcell to resist. John Gostling's bass voice must have been quite exceptional; and it may be imagined that the Chapel Royal at Whitehall was crowded by a fashionable congregation, headed by the king and his courtiers, eagerly anticipating the prospects of hearing some marvellous effect produced by the combined efforts of composer and singer, such as the following from *I will give thanks unto thee*:[1]

M

The declamation of this passage is perfect; and it is followed immediately by a phrase of extreme beauty in the richest register of the voice and within normal limits:

The repetition of the words 'shalt thou', one note higher and longer, to express the deep fervour of the appeal, is a touch of the highest artistry. Sometimes, however, the virtuoso passages written for Gostling have little to commend them, though they are interesting as records of the amazing flexibility and technical vocal control of this wonderful singer.

Of the anthems written for voices without independent accompaniment, two are of outstanding beauty: *Hear my prayer* and *Remember not, Lord, our offences. Hear my prayer,*[1] for eight voices, is constructed upon two brief phrases:

After a very quiet beginning the voices join in one by one in succession; and a wonderful climax is built up towards the close, where the treble voices for the first time reach the higher register. Though the anthem is clearly only a section of what was intended to be a longer work, it remains one of the finest examples in the repertory. It ends:

[1] *Purcell Society*, xxviii.

Remember not[1] has some very effective chromatic features.
Beginning in A minor, it has a full close in C major near the
end, and then follows a lovely phrase, quite simple, in block
harmony, modulating to F major:

Of the larger full anthems *O God, thou hast cast us out*[2] for six
voices is one of the best. The first section is in the contrapuntal
style of the late sixteenth century, although the harmonies and
progressions are mainly those of Purcell's time. The second
section opens with a verse passage treated antiphonally by
the three upper and the three lower voices; and the anthem
concludes with another contrapuntal chorus. *O Lord God of
hosts*,[3] for eight voices, is designed on rather similar lines, but
it is more academic in character. Burney found the second
section of this anthem 'extremely pathetic and expressive', but
he criticized the final section for 'experiments in harmony'
which gave him 'more pain than pleasure'.[4]

Most of the anthems with strings are laid out on extensive
lines, beginning with an overture. Many of these overtures are
of considerable length: the usual plan is to begin with a slow
movement in common measure breaking later into triple time,
much as Lully's overtures do. The words in almost all cases are
chosen from the Psalms. This is one of the features that mark a
fundamental difference between the Elizabethan anthem and
that of the Restoration period. The Elizabethans usually took
the Latin motet for their model, not only in the matter of
design but also in the choice of text. When they chose words
from the Psalms, a verse or two was all that was needed for

[1] *Purcell Society*, xxxii.   [2] *Purcell Society*, xxix.   [3] *Ibid.*
[4] *A General History of Music*, iii, p. 481.

their purpose, just as six lines of verse provided sufficient text
for a madrigal. If they wished to set several verses of a psalm
they joined together two or three compositions, complete in
themselves, labelling them Part i, Part ii, and so on. The
Restoration composers, by employing solo voices, trios and
quartets, as well as sections for full choir, had at their disposal
the means to deal with many verses, and even whole psalms. It
also happened that the psalms were very popular at this period;
and in a large number of instances Purcell, Blow and others
liked to begin at the first verse of a psalm and go steadily
through several verses in consecutive order.

The opening symphony of *O sing unto the Lord*[1] is of considerable length and begins with the same subject as the opening
bass solo. The second section is reminiscent of, though not
identical with, the quartet 'Sing unto the Lord and praise his
name'. The first entry of the chorus is delayed until the words
'Glory and worship are before him' are reached; it is then
made with great strength and is answered by the instruments.
After this comes an effective duet for treble and alto, constructed
on a simple figure which serves as a ground-bass throughout
this number and also for the *ritornello* that succeeds it; the
working-up of the subject by the strings to a final climax is
most effective. The feeling of mystery produced in the next
section is characteristic of Purcell's genius; it makes a striking
contrast to the joyous note of praise which runs through the
rest of this long anthem, particularly in the settings of 'The
beauty of holiness':

[1] *Purcell Society*, xvii.

With similar skill the spirit of awe is represented in the contra-puntal passage, clothed with chromatic harmonies, that follows.

Suddenly the bass soloist bursts in with the brilliant procla-mation 'Tell it out among the heathen', and the choir responds vigorously to each of his phrases. This movement provides a good example of Purcell's methods of dramatic expression, and there are also several touches of subtle realism. The rolling effect on the word 'round' will be obvious; but more subtle is the effect given to the word 'fast' by the rise of the fifth, with the note cut off by a semiquaver rest; and the laborious effort to push what 'cannot be moved' is wonderfully represented by the slurred notes in the concluding phrase:

fast   that it can - not be   moved.

The anthem ends with a rather long but splendid *Allelujah*, varied by verse, chorus and *ritornello*.

My heart is inditing[1] is the largest and the most important of all Purcell's anthems. It was sung at the coronation of James II at the moment when the queen, having been anointed and crowned, was conducted to the 'theatre' and seated on her throne beside the king. With a fine choir and orchestra at his disposal Purcell made full use of his opportunities to produce something on a grand scale.

The overture is on a bigger scale than that of any other Restoration anthem (Purcell used it again for his ode *Celestial Music*). It opens with a slow movement in square measure twenty-six bars long. This section is repeated and then followed by a brisk movement in triple time some forty bars in length. This also is marked to be repeated. There are no vocal solos in the anthem and the greater part of the choral work is for eight voices. These choruses are developed at far greater length than in Purcell's other anthems; they are grand examples of the finest type of contrapuntal writing. The choruses are accompanied by strings. Contrast and variety are secured by the setting of the section beginning 'She shall be brought unto the king', which is for six solo voices unaccompanied. A seventh voice joins in at the words 'with joy and gladness', and the composer has indicated 'quick' time at this point. Later an eight-part chorus develops the theme with string accompaniment. At its conclusion the overture is repeated in full.

A short octet of solo voices begins the verse 'Hearken, O daughter' and it is followed, with the same words, by a sextet

[1] *Purcell Society*, xvii.

ending with a *ritornello*. The sequence of massive discords towards the end of this movement is a magnificent example of Purcell's characteristic harmony:

The eight-part chorus 'Praise the Lord, O Jerusalem' gains in
dignity by being largely homophonic; it makes a glorious
climax to this great work. The *Alleluiah* that follows is in the
nature of a coda; it is also for eight voices and strings, and is
treated contrapuntally except for the concluding eight bars,
which, in block harmony, represent a final ecstatic acclamation,
the overwhelming effect of which can best be realized by those
who have been present in similar conditions in the Abbey at a
coronation ceremony.

O praise God in his holiness[1] is another fine anthem with
symphonies, though on a much smaller scale. An interesting
feature of this work is the independent combination of the

[1] *Purcell Society,* xiv.

second section of the overture with the opening chorus for four men's voices:

No more than passing mention can be made here of Purcell's skill in contrapuntal writing, as shown, for example, in the canon 5 and 1 in the anthem *Save me, O God*;[1] nor of the mystery which Purcell could impart to such a passage as 'Thou art he that took me out of my mother's womb' in the anthem *In thee, O Lord, do I put my trust*.[2] Equally remarkable is the following imaginative passage in *Praise the Lord, O my soul: O Lord my God*:[3]

---

[1] *Ibid.*, xiii.   [2] *Ibid.*, xiv.   [3] *Ibid.*, xvii.

-bled when thou tak-est a-way their breath they die, they

die —— and are turn-ed a-gain   to their dust.

Two further examples, both from verse sections, may be quoted to illustrate Purcell's harmonic procedures. The first is from *Let God arise*:[1]

The earth shook, ——|—— the earth shook ——

Here there is not only a picturesque interpretation of the word 'shook' but also the juxtaposition of two unrelated chords which had been used previously by Locke, and before him by Peri and Monteverdi, and which goes back ultimately to the Italian madrigal. The second example, from *Blessed is he that considereth the poor*,[2] shows what can happen when alto, tenor and bass are in close harmony:

---

[1] *Purcell Society*, xxviii.   [2] *Ibid.*

The text of the anthem *Thou knowest, Lord*[1] as performed at
the funeral of Queen Mary II in Westminster Abbey differs
from the familiar setting of this sentence[2] by Purcell in the
Burial Service. For this special occasion he added a dirge for
four 'flatt trumpetts' as a prelude, and a canzona at the end.
The effect was described by Tudway[3] as 'rapturously fine and
solemn'. Within a few months it was performed again at the
funeral of Purcell himself.

Compared with his anthems Purcell's two services are of no

---

[1] *Ibid.*, xxxii.   [2] *Ibid.*, xiii and xxix.
[3] British Museum, Harl. 7340, fo. 3.

great importance. The B♮ major Service[1] includes *Jubilate* as well as *Benedictus*, and *Cantate* and *Deus misereatur* as well as *Magnificat* and *Nunc dimittis*. It also includes a very fine and elaborate setting of *Benedicite* as an alternative to *Te Deum*. This *Benedicite*[2] is certainly the most interesting number in the service. The *Gloria* of *Magnificat* is written in canon 3 in 1, and that of *Nunc dimittis* in canon 4 in 2. This service, like the setting of the evening canticles in G minor,[3] might be said to suffer from too many verse passages. The magnificent *Te Deum* and *Jubilate* in D major[4] for five-part chorus, solo voices, trumpets and strings were composed for St Cecilia's Day 1694. They are on far too big a scale to be performed at a daily service: their place is at a festival.

DANIEL PURCELL (d. 1717), Henry's brother, was at one time organist of Magdalen College, Oxford, and later of St Andrew's, Holborn. An Evening Service of his in E minor was adapted for use by Sir John Stainer from a short organ-score without words. Some of his anthems survive in manuscript.

---

[1] *Purcell Society*, xxiii.
[3] *Purcell Society*, xxiii.
[2] Revised text in *Church Music Society*, No. 25.
[4] *Ibid.*

CHAPTER 14

The Beginning of the Eighteenth Century

The difficulty of grouping composers has already been mentioned. In the present chapter the grouping is based upon style rather than date, but both these considerations are dealt with somewhat elastically. The work of this group as a whole belongs to the beginning of the eighteenth century rather than to the end of the seventeenth.

The most important of these musicians is WILLIAM CROFT (1678–1727). He became a chorister of the Chapel Royal under Blow, whom he succeeded as organist of Westminster Abbey in 1708, having previously been organist of St Anne's, Soho. He was also Master of the Children of the Chapel Royal. He took the D.Mus. degree at Oxford in 1713.

He holds a unique position in English cathedral music by reason of his very beautiful setting of the Burial Service, the opening sentences of which are still sung at funerals. Croft stated[1] that in writing this service he 'endeavoured, as near as possibly I could', to imitate Purcell, and that he refrained from setting anew the sentence *Thou knowest, Lord* for reasons that would be 'obvious to every Artist'. Apart from this setting it cannot be said that much of his church music is of very high quality. His best work is shown in his 'occasional' music – for example, in his *Ode to Peace*, his odes for Queen Anne, and other such works. *The souls of the righteous* was composed for the funeral of Queen Anne in 1714. Other specially composed anthems were *I will give thanks* for the Thanksgiving Service after the battle of Blenheim in 1704, and *O give thanks*, with trumpets and strings, after the victory at Preston in 1715 – a work which falls below the standard set by Purcell, or even by

[1] Preface to *Musica Sacra*.

Turner and Tucker, for anthems of this kind. It includes a
florid alto solo with trumpet obbligato, beginning:

In 1724 Croft published 30 of his anthems, together with the Burial Service, in two volumes entitled *Musica Sacra*. Several of them still remain in use in cathedral choirs – for instance, *God is gone up with a merry noise,*[1] *Cry aloud and shout,*[2] *Sing praises to the Lord*[3] and *We will rejoice.*[4] Among less-known anthems *O Lord, thou hast searched me out*[5] includes two very long solos, one for bass and one for tenor, neither very distinguished. *Hear my prayer, O Lord, and let my crying*[5] is evidence of Croft's superiority in music of a pathetic cast:

---

[1] In *The Treasury of English Church Music, 1650–1760,* ed. C. Dearnley (Blandford Press).

[2] Ed. G. C. Martin (Novello).

[3] (Novello).

[4] (Novello).

[5] Ed. C. Hylton Stewart (Oxford University Press).

O Lord, rebuke me not[1] is perhaps the best of all his anthems. It opens in six parts followed by a short trio for alto, tenor and bass. The remainder of the anthem is for six voices, treated in imitation in two separate sections, ending with a contrapuntal *Amen*:

[1] Ed. C. Hylton Stewart (Oxford University Press).

It is strange that it should have been so neglected both in the past and the present.

Croft was one of the small group of composers who at about this period set to music *Sanctus* and *Gloria in excelsis*[1] for the Communion Office. This was in response to the demand for such settings created by the High Church movement in Queen Anne's reign. His Morning Service in A major[2] is still used in conjunction with a setting of the evening canticles which Stephen Elvey more than a century later wrote to be associated with it, incorporating some of Croft's material. The florid *Gloria* to *Jubilate*, which Elvey used again, is typical of the decadence which was already showing itself in the work of the eighteenth-century musicians. The many purposeless repetitions of certain passages, notably in the final verse of *Te Deum*, make a tiresome impression upon the listener.

JEREMIAH CLARKE (*c.* 1673–1707) was a chorister at the

---

[1] Printed in Arnold's *Cathedral Music*.
[2] (Novello).

Chapel Royal under Blow, and was in some way connected with St George's Chapel, Windsor,[1] where near relations of his were members of the choir. In 1692 he became organist of Winchester College, and in 1695 of St Paul's Cathedral. He died by his own hand.

Clarke composed the anthem *Praise the Lord*[2] for the coronation of Queen Anne. Another specially composed anthem was *The Lord is my strength*, 'for June 27th, 1706'.[3] He wrote various secular odes for special occasions, and an *Ode on the Assumption* which is in effect a sacred cantata. A good number of his anthems survive in manuscript. Boyce printed three in his *Cathedral Music*, including *I will love thee*[4] – a fine work very much in Purcell's manner. It includes a realistic setting for chorus of the words 'the earth trembled and quaked':

This is followed by a brilliant duet, in which the soloists sing of 'thunder, hailstones and coals of fire':

[1] E. H. Fellowes, *Organists . . . of St. George's Chapel*, p. 50.

[2] (Novello).

[3] This was the date of the Thanksgiving Service, held in St Paul's Cathedral and attended by Queen Anne, for the victory of Ramillies on May 12th and other recent successes. Both these dates are 'old style'.

[4] Ed. V. Novello (Novello).

There is a distinct Purcellian flavour in the final chorus:[1]

He shall send down from on high to fetch me, and shall take me out of ma – ny wa-ters: be-cause I have kept the ways of the Lord and have not for – sa – ken, for-sa – ken my God, and have not for – sa – ken, for – sa – ken my God, and have not for – sa-ken, for – sa – ken my God.

Clarke's setting of *Sanctus* and *Gloria in excelsis*,[2] like Croft's, is mainly written for men's voices. The full choir with boys enters at the words 'For thou only art holy'.

JOHN WELDON (1676–1736) was born at Chichester. He

---

[1] In *The Treasury of English Church Music, 1650–1760*, ed. C. Dearnley (Blandford Press).

[2] Printed in Arnold's *Cathedral Music*.

was a chorister at Eton College under John Walter. The
Bursar's Accounts show that Walter was allowed £5 at Michael-
mas 1693 'towards putting out Weldon the chorister for half a
year'. Other entries read: 'Paid for Weldon to Mr. H. Purcell
£1.10' in 1693–4, and 'allowed by the College to Mr. H.
Purcell with Weldon the chorister for half a year ended at
Lady Day 1694 £5'. It is clear from these entries that when his
voice broke Weldon was apprenticed to Purcell. In 1694 at the
age of 18 he became organist of St Bride's, Fleet Street, and
of St Martin's-in-the-Fields; and he succeeded John Blow as
organist of the Chapel Royal in 1708. He is best known now
by the two anthems which Boyce selected for his *Cathedral
Music: In thee, O Lord, have I put my trust*[1] and *Hear my crying.*[2]
Hear my crying is the better work of the two, though it suffers
from some rather conventional imitation and a general air of
amiability. The best section is the six-part verse 'I will dwell in
thy tabernacle', which swings along happily in triple time.
There is a touch of harmonic originality in the closing bars of
the final chorus:

Six of Weldon's anthems, written for Richard Elford, a
notable singer at the time, were published under the title
Divine Harmony. Several more survive in manuscript, including
an elaborate setting of *O praise the Lord* for treble and bass solos
and a trumpet obbligato (going to top C).[3]

Two cathedral dignitaries are among the composers of this
period: HENRY ALDRICH (1647–1710), canon (1681) and

[1] Ed. J. E. West (Bayley & Ferguson).
[2] *Church Music Society*, No. 39.   [3] Tenbury MS. 991.

subsequently Dean (1689) of Christ Church, Oxford, and ROBERT CREIGHTON, prebendary of Wells. Aldrich was a man of exceptionally versatile gifts. Educated on conventional classical lines at Westminster School and Christ Church, he became a notable theologian. His writings included a handbook on logic which became a classic, an *Epitome of Heraldry* and a treatise on architecture. As a practical architect he designed the Peckwater Quadrangle at Christ Church and All Saints' Church, Oxford. He was also a competent musician, though not of outstanding ability as a composer. His anthems *Out of the deep* and *O give thanks*, and his Service in G major (including *Sanctus* and *Gloria*) were printed in Boyce's *Cathedral Music*. They are still to be heard occasionally. The Dean's musicianship led him in another direction: he was a collector of rare music-books, both printed and manuscript. His splendid collection was bequeathed by him to Christ Church, where it provides one of the most valuable fields in this country for musical research. Aldrich developed a curious accomplishment which would seem to have been more attractive to him than original composition. This was to rewrite or adapt or enlarge the anthems and other works of earlier composers. Farrant's *Hide not thou thy face* was converted from a four-part to an eight-part composition. He was especially fond of adapting the works of Carissimi. It was Aldrich, too, in another connexion, who first adapted the latter part of the Litany as a continuation of Tallis's setting, using the material of Tallis's *Versicles and Responses*. This adaptation was made in the first instance for the Latin version of the English Prayer Book version of the Litany.

ROBERT CREIGHTON (*c.* 1639–1734), as his name and that of his father is usually spelt in preference to Creyghton, was also a distinguished scholar. Like his father, who was Dean of Wells, he also was Professor of Greek at Cambridge. He became a canon of Wells in 1674 and held this position until the end of his very long life. His music is undistinguished, though his short anthem *I will arise*,[1] a rather academic piece, still holds its place in cathedral choirs.

JAMES HAWKINS (d. 1729) was organist of Ely Cathedral

---

[1] Ed. G. Bantock (Curwen).

from 1681 until his death. He wrote as many as 17 services and 75 anthems. Nothing of his now survives in use, but he did important work in transcribing church music of the sixteenth and seventeenth centuries, and his collection at Ely has been of considerable value to modern editors.

JOHN GOLDWIN (*c.* 1667–1719), or Golding as he should more correctly be called, was Child's pupil and successor at Windsor. He wrote a number of anthems and a Service in F major. *I have set God alway before me*[1] was printed by Boyce and is occasionally sung, but it is an indifferent work.

DANIEL ROSEINGRAVE (*c.* 1650–1727) is another musician of this period who wrote a good deal of church music, little of which is now extant even in manuscript. He was organist of St Patrick's Cathedral and Christ Church, Dublin, having previously been at Gloucester, Winchester and Salisbury Cathedrals. His son THOMAS (1690–1766) was a more notable musician. He was appointed the first organist of St George's, Hanover Square, in 1725. Though he wrote a few anthems his most important compositions were for the harpsichord and organ. RALPH (*c.* 1695–1747), another son of Daniel, succeeded his father as organist of Christ Church, Dublin. He wrote some anthems and services.

HENRY HALL (1655–1707) was a chorister of the Chapel Royal. He became organist of Exeter Cathedral in 1674 and of Hereford in 1688. In conjunction with WILLIAM HINE (1687–1730), a pupil of Jeremiah Clarke, who became organist of Gloucester Cathedral in 1710 he wrote a Morning Service known as 'Hall and Hine in E♭'.[2] This very dull and uninspired work was allowed by undiscriminating precentors and organists to keep a place in cathedral lists until the close of the nineteenth century.

---

[1] (Novello).
[2] Printed in Arnold's *Cathedral Music*.

CHAPTER 15

Early Georgian Composers

The dominating figure in English musical life in the first half of the eighteenth century was Handel. His stature was so considerable that he largely dwarfed the English-born musicians of his time. In consequence it has often been said that his influence had a crushing effect on native talent. This explanation of the relative poverty of English music at this time will clearly not hold water. Gifted composers are not crushed by others with gifts equal or superior to their own. The brutal truth is that English composers were inferior to Handel and seem to have made little effort to rise above that inferiority.

GEORGE FRIDERIC HANDEL (1685–1759), as he spelled his name in England, was born at Halle, now in East Germany, where he served his apprenticeship as a church organist. Migrating to Hamburg in 1703, he discovered the world of opera and also his own talent for the stage. In Italy he won success as an opera composer, and achieved equal success when he came to London in 1710. For the rest of his life London was his home, and he became a naturalized Englishman in 1726. The eventual failure of his operatic enterprises induced him to turn to oratorio, which reached a wider public and proved to be more profitable. Though he liked to visit St Paul's Cathedral and play the organ there, he wrote nothing for the regular services of the English church. His *Chandos Anthems*, written during the early years of his residence in England, are cantatas, designed for the particular circumstances of his patron's chapel, and the style is predominantly German or Italian or a mixture of both. His other compositions for the church were written for special occasions, such as the four anthems for the coronation of George II, where his mastery of the 'grand' style produced splendid results, or the funeral anthem for Queen Caroline. None of these works, much less the *Dettingen Te Deum*, is suitable for ordinary cathedral use, though *Zadok the priest* has been heard at other coronations beyond the one for which it was first written. Any detectable influence of English church music in these works can be regarded only as incidental: Handel was too well grounded in Continental traditions to accept what was to some extent a parochial style, though in opera and the lighter moments of his oratorios he showed that he was not insensitive to English popular song. There, is, however, one striking passage in *Israel in Egypt* where he borrowed the manner of the Restoration verse anthem – the chorus 'He sent thick darkness', which obviously made an impression on Mendelssohn, who used the same methods in *Elijah*.

Among Handel's near contemporaries the two most important were Maurice Greene and William Boyce.

MAURICE GREENE (*c.* 1695–1755) was the son of a London clergyman. His grandfather John Greene was Recorder of the City of London. He was a chorister at St Paul's Cathedral and succeeded Daniel Purcell as organist of St Andrew's, Holborn, in 1717. In 1727 he was appointed organist of St Paul's. In 1730 he was chosen Professor of Music at Cambridge University and received the degree of Mus.D.

In his early days at St Paul's he came into close touch with Handel. There are many stories associated with their relationship and their subsequent estrangement; but the influence of Handel is conspicuous in Greene's two volumes of 40 anthems, published in 1743. His music shows a kind of facility which suggests that many of the anthems were written without sufficient trouble, in accordance with a formula. For example, numbers of the solo anthems open with a bass passage (figured for full accompaniment) made up of short musical phrases treated sequentially, e.g. the opening section of the Christmas anthem, *Behold, I bring you glad tidings*, is largely based on a sequential figure of this kind:

A similar weakness that suggests a lack of effort by the composer is found in the first section of the Epiphany anthem *Arise, shine*,[1] in which the voices are accompanied by a persistent rhythmical figure in the bass of the accompaniment:

[1] In *The Treasury of English Church Music, 1650–1760*, ed. C. Dearnley (Blandford Press).

On the other hand the relentless tread of the crotchet bass in
Lord, let me know mine end,[1] which was sung at Nelson's funeral
in St Paul's Cathedral, is impressive, and there is a simple
pathos in the final section:

---

[1] Ed. E. Bullock (Oxford University Press).

Greene was at his best with the full anthem without independent accompaniment. *O clap your hands together*,[1] for five voices, is a first-rate piece of work. It is designed on a well-balanced scheme; each verse of the psalm is set in a contrapuntal manner in a separate section, although the main continuity of the chorus is not broken. A climax is gradually worked up at the words 'sing praises unto our God' with a figure of rapid notes taken up in turn by one voice after another with brilliant effect. Then comes a full close and a rest, after which all the voices join in a homophonic passage, four bars long, proclaiming twice the supreme thought of the psalm: 'For God is the King of all the earth':

[1] In *The Treasury of English Church Music, 1650–1760*, ed. C. Dearnley (Blandford Press).

The effect is as if these words stood out from the rest of the psalm in capital letters. The anthem ends with further acclamations of praise, expressed in rapid phrases treated contrapuntally. *How long wilt thou forget me, O Lord?* is an eight-part anthem containing many fine passages. Contrast is provided by a brief duet for two trebles.

The verse anthems can be dealt with only briefly; and out of so many only a few can be selected for comment. In spite of the caustic observation attributed to Handel that he hung up Greene's anthems out of doors 'because they wanted air', Greene showed a fair gift for melody. One of his most beautiful solos is 'I will lay me down in peace' in the anthem *O God of my righteousness*:[1]

[1] Ed. J. E. West (Novello).

Equally effective is the tenor solo from 'Thou visitest the earth' in the anthem *Thou, O God, art praised in Sion*. The long alto solo that precedes it is not of the same quality. The design of this anthem is typical of Greene's work. It opens with an alto and tenor duet, followed by the alto solo just mentioned. Then comes another long duet for alto and tenor, with some descriptive phrases expressing 'the raging of the sea', 'the noise of his waves' and 'the madness of the people'. The full choir is employed only at the end to repeat the material of the tenor

solo. It is evident that in Greene's time the alto voice was still a
great feature of cathedral music. It is prominent in *God is our
hope and strength*[1] and again in *Acquaint thyself with God*,[2] not only
in the two sections at the beginning, but in the florid aria 'Then
shall he be thy defence', which follows. This is among the best
of Greene's solos, with a strong rhythm and a fine spirit. The
opening aria has a very attractive obbligato for a solo stop on
the organ. The short chorus that ends this anthem is rather
laboured. *Let God arise*,[3] laid out on a large plan, has some
fine moments but is unequal in merit. The best movement is
for verse and chorus alternately, set to the words 'like as the
smoke vanisheth'.

In addition to Greene's 40 published anthems Arnold printed
a further eight in his *Cathedral Music*; a few more survive
in manuscript. Greene wrote a Service in C major (*Te Deum,
Jubilate, Magnificat* and *Nunc Dimittis*) which contains sections
for six and eight voices, varied with verse passages. It is a very
uneven work. The eight-part writing at the words 'Day by day'
in *Te Deum*, for instance, is fine; but in contrast the eight-part
Gloria of *Nunc dimittis* is poor in material and unsatisfactory in
accentuation, e.g.:

[1] (Novello).
[2] Ed. C. Hylton Stewart (Oxford University Press).
[3] (Novello).

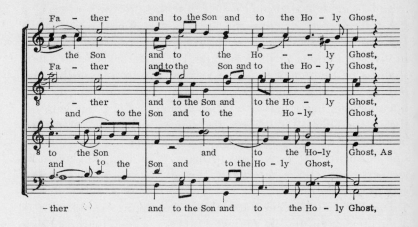

Greene was a pupil of CHARLES KING (1687–1748), who was a chorister at St Paul's Cathedral under Blow, and later under Jeremiah Clarke, whose sister he married. He was organist of St Benet Fink and a lay-clerk of St Paul's. He is best known for his services in C major and F major,[1] which are, however, of small musical value. A passage in the F major *Te Deum*, 'We believe that thou shalt come', is similar to 'Smiling meadows seem to say' in Wilbye's madrigal *Flora gave me fairest flowers*, not merely in melodic material but also in contrapuntal treatment:

WILBYE

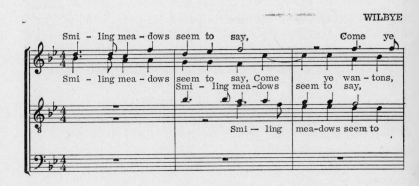

[1] (Novello).

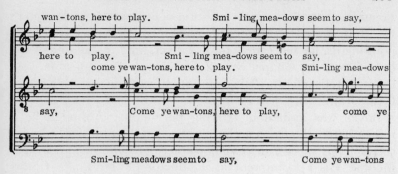

King wrote as many as six services and a few anthems. It was his pupil Greene who originated the comment that 'King was a serviceable man'. His services were no better and no worse than the many others produced at this period which occupied so large a place in cathedral lists until the close of the nineteenth century.

WILLIAM BOYCE (1710–79) was about fifteen years younger than Greene and outlived him by more than twenty; but owing to his deafness he gave up composition many years before his death and his music dates almost entirely before the accession of George III. He was the son of the beadle of the Worshipful Company of Joiners and was a chorister at St Paul's Cathedral. He was subsequently articled to Greene and later studied under

Pepusch. After holding the position of organist at St Michael's Cornhill, and All Hallows, Thames Street, among other appointments, he succeeded John Travers in 1758 as one of the organists of the Chapel Royal. The later years of his life were spent in retirement at Kensington. He was buried in St Paul's Cathedral.

Boyce was a man of striking personality. Although he is remembered chiefly as a church musician he also worked with conspicuous success in secular music, both choral and instrumental. His appointment as conductor of the Three Choirs Festival (Gloucester, Hereford and Worcester) in 1737 is especially interesting from a historical point of view. It is recorded[1] that it was his custom 'to mark the measure to the orchestra with a roll of parchment or paper in hand'. He was thus one of the first conductors in England to adopt the modern method of conducting with the equivalent of a baton. For many years after this the usual practice was for the leading violinist to direct the orchestra. A story is told of Philip Hayes at the Handel Festival of 1784.[2] He had come to give his assistance as one of the conductors by beating time. 'When the time of the performance had arrived, and Mr. Cramer, the leader, had just tapt his bow (the signal for being ready), and looked round to catch the eyes of the performers, he saw to his astonishment a tall gigantic figure . . . with a roll of parchment in his hand. "Who is that gentleman?" said Mr. Cramer. "Dr. Hayes," was the reply. "Be so kind", said Mr. Cramer, "to tell the gentleman that when he has sat down I will begin." Hayes thereupon sat down and Cramer went on unhindered.' Boyce held the appointment as conductor of the Three Choirs Festival until precluded by his deafness.

The form of the cathedral anthem had become definitely established by the middle of the eighteenth century. It is well represented in Boyce's work in such anthems as *O where shall wisdom be found?*[3] and *I have surely built thee an house.*[4] It is the 'short cantata' form, consisting of several movements, including

---

[1] Lecture by Samuel Wesley in 1827 (see Grove's *Dictionary, s.v.* Conducting).
[2] W. T. Parke, *Musical Memoirs*, i, p. 39.
[3] (Novello).   [4] Ed. V. Novello (Novello).

sections for chorus, verse and solo. This was the model that
was being evolved by the Restoration composers; it was also
the model upon which S. S. Wesley worked in the nineteenth
century. The big-scale anthem did not, however, exclude the
full anthem, whether short or extended. Boyce left examples in
all these forms.

The two anthems just mentioned stand out above the rest of
Boyce's work, and indeed they take a high place among the
classic examples of English cathedral music. There are several
details in *O where shall wisdom be found?* of such subtle artistry
that some doubt is raised as to whether this anthem can really
be entirely the work of Boyce. Similar doubts arise in connexion
with *I have surely built thee an house.* For Boyce could and did
write much, both in his sacred and secular work, that is no
more than moderately good, and much also that is poor; so
that, making ample allowance for the varying quality found
in the work even of the greatest composers, it is difficult to
explain the touch of genius which certain of his anthems do
occasionally display, side by side with so much that is commonplace and conventional. A suggestion may be submitted here
in full knowledge that no evidence whatever can be produced
to support it. Are some of these anthems, as they stand, not
entirely the work of Boyce? It is not irrelevant to point out that
none of his anthems were published in his lifetime: the two
volumes were 'printed for the Author's widow' in 1780 and
1790 after his death. It is also a fact that he collected much
material by earlier composers to print in his three volumes of
Cathedral Music. This must have included many more works for
which he could find no room in his final selection. Moreover,
he stated himself that much of the text as he found it needed
correction; consequently a quantity of anthems might have
been found in his portfolios after his death written out in his
own hand, but not necessarily composed by him, and some of
them probably not labelled with any composer's name. Were
those who put together these two volumes quite certain about
Boyce's authorship in every instance? Were any of the works
possibly adaptations of Restoration compositions, like the
adaptations that Aldrich in his time made of earlier works?

No one now can say; but more than one musician has been troubled with doubt on this point.

In *O where shall wisdom?* the verbal accentuation throughout the anthem is admirable. An unusually subtle touch of realism is shown in the opening verse in the *weighing* of the silver:

The emphasis given by the repetition of the word 'where' in the first question: 'Where? – *where* shall wisdom be found?' is again found in the further question 'Where? – *where* is the place of understanding?' Later comes the answer 'then – *then* did he see it and prepare it'. The inquiry becomes more persistent in the contrapuntal passage 'Whence then cometh wisdom?', and the climax is reached in a strong phrase in block harmony with the final question 'where is the place of understanding?' This phrase closes on the dominant of C minor and then a sudden feeling of mystery and awe is expressed in E♭ major. With great dramatic force the full choir bursts in, solemnly proclaiming that 'God understandeth the way thereof':

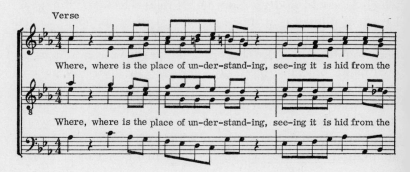

eyes of all | liv–ing? God un–der–stand–eth the way there–of.

eyes of all | liv–ing? God un–der–stand–eth the way there–of.

The dramatic character of the anthem is sustained in the trio that follows, notably at the D♭ chord in the high register for the lightning. Finally comes God's answer to man, expressed first by a male-voice trio, and finally by the chorus with its clear-cut phrases 'that, *that* is wisdom', and 'that is understanding'. The quality of this chorus is markedly inferior to the rest of the anthem; it contrasts unfavourably with the solemn utterance of the preceding trio.

Boyce also fails to maintain a consistently high level of excellence throughout the anthem *I have surely built thee an house*. Here again, however, the verbal accentuation is uniformly true. The opening recitative is typical. The bass voice builds up his first phrase quite simply until he reaches C on the words 'house' and 'place'. The emphatic value of the tenor E on the word 'indeed' also shows an imaginative response to the text:

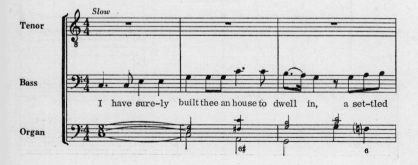

I have sure–ly built thee an house to dwell in, a set–tled

The influence here is Purcellian, as it is in *O where shall wisdom be found?* There is a Purcellian flavour also in the male-voice trio that follows. The phrase 'when thou hearest forgive', with which a later trio concludes, is especially beautiful:

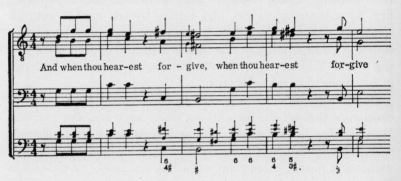

The tenor recitative 'If there be in the land famine' is another piece of expressive declamation, full of pathos and fervour:

The pompous *tasto solo* and recitative that follows at the words 'And the Lord said to Solomon', although the diction is admirable, seems to be by another hand altogether. So also does the commonplace 'Halleluiah' with which the anthem ends. Can it be that this work of high imagination and admirable craftsmanship is by one of the Restoration composers, adapted and completed by Boyce? If this is entirely his work he deserves to be regarded as one of the outstanding composers of English church music.

The Heavens declare the glory of God opens with an effective chorus for men's voices, but as a whole is an uneven work. *Turn thee unto me* opens admirably with a very expressive five-part chorus that can be sung unaccompanied, followed by a charming duet for treble voices. The final movement is less successful; the florid phrase on the word 'confounded' is out of character with the subject. There is some effective eight-part writing in

O give thanks. By the waters of Babylon is well written, and the opening movement creates the right atmosphere, but a duet for two trebles is an inadequate medium for the taunt 'Sing us one of the songs of Sion'. Very few of the rest of the anthems are worth performing today.

Of Boyce's services, that in C major has many good qualities and is far superior to the numerous services in short form which were written in the eighteenth century. The verbal accentuation is particularly good, and the phrases are not made subservient to any regular measures of four or eight bars. In these respects it is superior to the Short Service in A major. Why Boyce limited his settings to *Te Deum* and *Jubilate* is not known. Samuel Arnold wrote an Evening Service for use with Boyce's Short Service in A. For his *Te Deum* in G major Philip Hayes wrote a *Jubilate*.

Boyce's name will always be associated with his three volumes of *Cathedral Music*. This famous collection, however, was not his work alone. It was his master, Maurice Greene, who first planned it. While he was doing so it came to the notice of John Alcock, Organist of Lichfield Cathedral, who had already embarked on a similar undertaking. Alcock generously placed his work at Greene's disposal. Greene had not completed the task when he died, and he bequeathed his materials to Boyce, under whose editorship the three volumes were published in the years 1760, 1768 and 1773. The volumes are fine specimens of the engraver's art; and the curious designs printed at the end of some of the compositions are characteristic of the period. These designs, some of which are elaborate representations of birds, fishes and other grotesque figures, are produced by a single unbroken line, drawn without once raising the pen from the paper.

The other composers of this period need be only briefly noticed. WILLIAM HAYES (1707–77) was organist of Worcester Cathedral and afterwards of Magdalen College, Oxford. He became Professor of Music at Oxford in 1742. He wrote a good number of anthems, including *Great is the Lord*, *O worship the Lord* and *Praise the Lord*, none of which achieve any distinction. His services have passed into oblivion.

THOMAS KELWAY (d. 1749) belonged to a Windsor family connected with St George's Chapel. He became organist of Chichester Cathedral in 1720. His anthems are now forgotten. Of his evening services that in B minor is the best known; it is an indifferent work, with too many repeated closes in D major. There is also an Evening Service in A major at Durham and a Morning and Evening Service in F major with *Cantate* and *Deus misereatur* at Chichester.

JOHN TRAVERS (1706–58) began his career as a chorister of St George's Chapel, Windsor, and became organist of the Chapel Royal in 1737. His familiar Morning and Evening Service in F major[1] has little to commend it when compared with the many fine settings that are available of the Short Service type. Of his anthems *Ascribe unto the Lord*[2] deserves to be remembered. There is much individuality in the baritone solo beginning 'Let the heavens rejoice'. From first to last it overflows with joy, while in florid passages both voice and organ tell how 'all the trees of the wood rejoice before the Lord':

---

[1] (Novello).

[2] In *The Treasury of English Church Music, 1650–1760*, ed. C. Dearnley (Blandford Press).

This florid accompaniment is reputed to have been written to show off what was called the 'mounted cornett' stop. Its use was much in fashion in Travers's time; it was a kind of 'mixture' with several ranks of pipes to a note.

CHARLES STROUD died in 1726 when not more than 20 years old. There is good reason to think that his proved ability would have carried him far had he lived. His anthem *Hear my prayer*, which is still sung in many cathedrals, certainly gives proof of his promising gifts as a composer.

JAMES KENT (1700–76) was a pupil of Vaughan Richardson, and like him became organist of Winchester Cathedral. For a long period his anthems and his Service in D major enjoyed great popularity. *Hear my prayer*[1] was an especial favourite, a feature of it being the duet for two trebles. It was sung at the funeral of George III in St George's Chapel, and again at the funeral of George IV, when it was stated to have been 'a favourite one of the late King'.[2] In fact Kent was one of the poorest of all the eighteenth-century composers, and his music is deservedly forgotten.

THOMAS KEMPTON (d. 1762), organist of Ely Cathedral from 1729, is remembered for his Morning and Evening Service in B♭ major – one of the best of the eighteenth-century Short Services.

JAMES NARES (1715–83) was a musician of some distinction, notably as a composer of music for the harpsichord and the organ. He also wrote a treatise on singing and some secular music. He was appointed organist of York Minster at the age of 19 and later became organist of the Chapel Royal. His church music is of much less value than his other work. His Morning and Evening Service in F major resembles many other eighteenth-century services in its lack of inspiration and its academic character. Of his anthems *The souls of the righteous, O Lord my God* and *Try me, O God* are useful as short works for morning use.

Apart from the work of Greene and Boyce, who were essentially anthem-writers, this period of cathedral music is remarkable for the number of services written, though as a whole they represent by far the dullest group in the entire repertory of the settings of the English canticles. The choice of words for anthems, as in the Restoration period, was almost entirely restricted to the Psalms. Boyce's two finest anthems *O where shall wisdom be found?* and *I have surely built* are among the very few exceptions. *Behold I bring you glad tidings* is almost the only exception in Greene's large output. William Hayes and Nares kept mainly to the Psalms; Kent went further afield with *When the Son of man shall come, Who is this that cometh from Edom?* and *Blessed be thou, Lord God*. None of these composers seem to have set collects.

---

[1] (Novello).
[2] *The Times*, 15 July 1830.

CHAPTER 16

Later Georgian Composers

This period, which may be taken to extend roughly from the accession of George III to that of Queen Victoria, is a very lean one in the history of English cathedral music. Only three names are to be found here that rise even to the level of mediocrity: Jonathan Battishill, Thomas Attwood and Samuel Wesley.

JONATHAN BATTISHILL (1738–1801) was a chorister at St Paul's Cathedral under William Savage, to whom he was afterwards articled as an organ pupil. His attention was then turned to secular song rather than to church music, and he became closely associated with Arne, whose influence is shown in some of his anthems, for instance, in the baritone solo 'O go your way' in *Behold how good and joyful*, and in the duet 'And he hath put a new song in my mouth' in *I waited patiently*. That he had great talent is shown by his two anthems *O Lord, look down from heaven*[1] and *Call to remembrance*.[2] *O Lord, look down from heaven* is worthy of a place among the best full anthems in the repertory. The words are chosen not from the Psalms but from the Book of Isaiah. It is dated 5 June 1765 in John Page's edition of Battishill's anthems published in 1804. It opens quietly with three voices and then four, treated in imitation; a second treble part is added at the words 'where is thy zeal and thy strength?' and shortly afterwards a second bass part is added. This device for the gradual reinforcement of the volume of tone postpones the necessity for more than a slight *crescendo* until the climax of the appeal is approached. Then the voices, after a rest, sing detached phrases in block harmony with increasing force and emotion, producing their fullest effect in

[1] Ed. G. C. Martin (Novello).
[2] (Novello).

the repetition of the words 'thy mercies towards me'. At this point the composer, with a touch of very fine artistry, gives a whole bar's silence followed by a profoundly moving treatment of the words 'are they restrained?' It would be difficult to find a more beautiful dramatic effect than that secured here by the simplest means in the handling of voices:

Call to remembrance is another first-rate anthem of a penitential character. It opens with a beautiful piece of five-part writing, followed by a verse passage for seven voices which answer each other in groups of three and four, and this is rounded off by the full choir in seven parts. The anthem is a little spoiled by the prolongation of the second half, beginning with the words 'O remember not the sins'. This verse of the psalm is given first to a trio of solo voices and repeated with the same melodic material in the subsequent chorus. This chorus is mainly in seven parts, smoothly written and very vocal. Battishill obviously knew the value of the octave as an interval in vocal writing.

SAMUEL WESLEY (1766–1837) was a man of very wide culture; he was a classical scholar, a good linguist and had a fine taste in literature. In addition to these accomplishments he was an exceptionally good musician. In music, too, his gifts were displayed in many different branches of the art. He was considered the greatest organist of his time, with an exceptional skill in *extempore* playing. He was also a good violinist, and his little-known violin concertos[1] reveal an admirable and intimate knowledge of violin technique. Besides all these things he was a notable composer. Orchestral music, chamber music, organ and pianoforte works, oratorios, Masses, songs and glees are

[1] British Museum, Add. 35,008, fo. 60.

among his compositions, in addition to his English church music. He was born at Bristol, the son of Charles Wesley, the hymn-writer, and nephew of John Wesley. (His elder brother Charles, who also had considerable musical gifts, wrote some anthems and was organist of St Marylebone Church.) The small amount of his English church music may be accounted for by the fact that in early life he joined the Church of Rome. Two motets, with alternative Latin and English words, are two of the best pieces of cathedral music produced in this period. *In exitu Israel* (*When Israel came out of Egypt*) is for double chorus. It is noteworthy that Wesley earned a very high reputation as a performer of Bach's organ and harpsichord works and that he did much to make Bach's works known in England. A telling effect is produced where all the voices join in unison at the phrase 'Jordanis conversus est retrorsum', with an extended florid run on the last word. *Exultate Deo* (*Sing aloud with gladness*), for five voices, is similar in character, admirably vocal and brilliant in effect. It is constructed upon two main phrases:

(a) Ex-ul - ta - te De - o ad-ju - to - ri nos - tro
Sing a-loud with glad-ness un-to God our help - er

(b) Su - mi-te psal - mum, et da - te tym-pa-num
Come ye with mu - sic, strike ye the ta - bou-ret

Thou, O God, art praised in Sion is a four-part motet with English words only. Like the two big motets just mentioned it is developed mainly on the opening theme, which, once more, is first given out by the bass voices in unison. The anthem *All go unto one place* was written for the funeral of Wesley's brother Charles in 1834.

THOMAS ATTWOOD (1765–1838) was a smaller man, but not without talent. He began his career as a Chapel Royal chorister. Under the patronage of the Prince of Wales (afterwards George IV) he was sent to study music in Naples, and after two years there went to Vienna as a pupil of Mozart. The record of his studies, with Mozart's corrections,[1] makes an illuminating study. Returning to England Attwood continued in royal favour and held various appointments connected with the Court. In 1796 he became organist of St Paul's Cathedral, and for a short time before his death he was organist of the Chapel Royal.

In early life he devoted his attention mainly to dramatic work; he turned to church music at a later period. As many as four of his services were published after his death, together with eight anthems. Of the services that in F major was the most popular, but the composer seems too often to have been bound by the convention of writing regular phrases of four bars; the repetitions of words required for the rounding off of many of these phrases are often tiresome and meaningless, and his verbal accentuation is not always true, e.g.:

[1] *Neue Mozart-Ausgabe*, Ser. X, Werkgruppe 30, Bd. 1, ed. D. Heartz & A. Mann (Bärenreiter).

His short anthems are unpretentious; but *Come, Holy Ghost,* *Turn thy face from my sins* and *Teach me, O Lord,* which is part of a longer work, deserve the popularity which they still enjoy. Attwood wrote two coronation anthems with orchestral accompaniment; *I was glad* was for the coronation of George IV, and *O Lord, grant the king a long life* for William IV. *I was glad,* a pretentious piece, was repeated at Queen Victoria's coronation.

The rest of the composers classified under this heading may be dismissed with brief notices.

PHILIP HAYES (1738–97) was the son of William Hayes. Like his father he became Professor of Music at Oxford and organist of Magdalen College, having been formerly organist of New College. He wrote a *Jubilate* to be sung with Boyce's *Te Deum* in G major, and a few anthems, including *The Lord descended.* His encounter with Cramer at the Handel Commemoration has already been mentioned.[1]

JOHN ALCOCK (1715–1806) was a chorister at St Paul's Cathedral, and became organist of Lichfield Cathedral in 1750. He wrote a large number of anthems and a Service in E minor. His work in collecting material for an edition of cathedral music was mentioned in the previous chapter.[2] In the course of his researches Alcock became acquainted with Byrd's Great Service, and his score[3] shows that the alto and bass Decani parts were already missing from the available text.

BENJAMIN COOKE (1734–93), a pupil of Pepusch, became organist of Westminster Abbey in 1762. His flamboyant Evening Service in G major was composed for a special occasion in the Abbey. His son ROBERT (1768–1814) was organist of Westminster Abbey from 1802 until his death. His Evening Service in C major is his only piece of church music of any note.

THOMAS EBDON (1738–1816) became Organist of Durham in 1763. His Service in C major has already been mentioned[4] as including *Sanctus* and *Gloria in excelsis.* Two volumes of his cathedral music were published, one in 1790 and the second in 1810.

THOMAS NORRIS (1741–90) is remembered only by his

[1] p. 202.
[2] p. 208.
[3] British Museum, Add. 31,443, fo. 98.
[4] p. 29.

anthem *Hear my prayer*, a work of little interest. He had some repute as a tenor and composed six symphonies.

SAMUEL WEBBE (1740–1816) earned a great reputation as a glee-writer. Being a Roman Catholic he wrote little for the Anglican Church, but *The Lord is the portion of mine inheritance* is still sometimes sung.

JOHN CLARKE, afterwards known as Clarke-Whitfeld (1770–1836), was a pupil of Philip Hayes. In 1793 he became organist of St Patrick's Cathedral and Christ Church, Dublin, and in 1820 organist of Hereford Cathedral. He was a voluminous composer and his church music was once very popular. Of his services that in E major has rather more to commend it than the rest. *In Jewry is God known* and *Behold how good and joyful* are two of his anthems which may be picked out from a large number of quite undistinguished compositions.

WILLIAM CROTCH (1775–1847) held a prominent position in the English musical world: he was Professor of Music at Oxford and was also the first Principal of the Royal Academy of Music. He was an astonishing infant prodigy, and is said to have given a series of daily pianoforte recitals in London at the age of four. His church music is slight in bulk. The best of his anthems is *How dear are thy counsels*, which is a graceful piece of writing and happy in the recapitulation of the first subject near the end. The oratorio *Palestine* is a work of some importance historically, for it is the only even moderately outstanding English oratorio between Arne's *Judith* and Sterndale Bennett's *Woman of Samaria*. Two choruses from this work – *Lo, star-led chiefs* and *Be peace on earth* – have been adopted as anthems.

It remains to mention SAMUEL ARNOLD (1740–92), a notable personality in English musical circles in the period that preceded Crotch and Wesley. He became a chorister in the Chapel Royal under Bernard Gates, and later under Nares. For many years he devoted his abilities to dramatic music and to oratorio, his most notable work being *The Prodigal Son*. In the course of time he was appointed organist of the Chapel Royal, and in 1793 he succeeded Benjamin Cooke as organist of Westminster Abbey. He wrote little church music, but his three volumes of *Cathedral Music*, to which a fourth was added to include the organ parts, were a valuable contribution to the repertory of available anthems and services at a time when cheap octavo editions were unknown.

An important innovation was introduced at this period which has had a lasting effect upon the construction of the weekly music-lists of cathedral choirs. Theodore Aylward (1730–1801) first introduced the custom of choosing excerpts from Handel's *Messiah* and other such works for performance as anthems in the choir of St George's Chapel, Windsor. He was not primarily a church musician, though he held appointments as organist of St Lawrence, Jewry, and St Michael's, Cornhill, before going to Windsor. In 1784 he took a leading part in organizing the Handel Commemoration, held in Westminster Abbey on a scale unprecedented at that time. Four years later at the age of 58 he was appointed to St George's Chapel and so had to exercise the choice of music for the daily services. The innovation of singing choruses from *Messiah* spread through the cathedrals very quickly and the choice was extended to other oratorios of Handel. It was not long before excerpts from the works of Mozart also came into use, and this field was enormously widened in the course of the nineteenth century, not only through the inclusion of music by Bach, Mendelssohn and Brahms but also through the introduction of works by Palestrina and other Continental composers of the sixteenth century.

CHAPTER 17

Early Victorian Composers

By the time Queen Victoria ascended the throne in 1837 the music of Haydn, Mozart and Beethoven had become widely known in England and was not without influence on cathedral music. During the early Victorian period there were those, such as G. J. Elvey and F. A. G. Ouseley, who still held to conservative ideas and to older methods. T. A. Walmisley and more particularly S. S. Wesley represent the advance guard, looking with clear vision into the future. John Goss stands half-way between these two influences. J. B. Dykes is another conspicuous figure in this group, who first led the way to a new form of emotional expression in church music.

The output of cathedral music greatly increased during the first years of Victoria's reign and rapidly grew to enormous proportions. Two contributing factors may be mentioned. One was the coming of cheap printed music produced in octavo editions. The credit for this is due to the firm of Novello & Co., founded in 1811 by Vincent Novello. The credit for originating the idea, in the face of much difficulty at the time, belongs to Joseph Alfred Novello about the year 1830. The cost of printed vocal music during the early years of Victoria's reign was thus reduced to about a twentieth of the former cost. This was an immense boon to singers and composers alike: it led to the formation of choral societies throughout the towns and villages, and greatly stimulated the activities of composers both of secular and sacred music.

The other cause for the increased output of church music was the Oxford Movement, which dates from 1834. This led very soon to the establishment of surpliced choirs in a great number of parish churches and a consequent demand for services and anthems in many of them, especially in large town parishes where it became the fashion, on Sunday evenings, to aim at musical services on cathedral lines. At a later period the parish churches rather than the cathedrals led the way to the choral celebration of the Holy Communion; this created a demand which was in due course met with a huge output of music.

It is often said that Victorian church music was of a very inferior quality, tainted with sentimentalism, and that it suffered from this taint until rescued from it by Stanford and Parry. If the facts are carefully examined it will be seen that after the very lean period, extending over a hundred years, which has been described in the two previous chapters, a great revival took place in the early years of Victoria. Sebastian Wesley and the younger Walmisley were in early manhood at the time of the queen's accession, and Goss was 36. Elvey was already organist of St George's Chapel. None of these composers could be described as sentimentalists, even if, admittedly, they were not all greatly gifted. Furthermore the older music of Purcell and his contemporaries, together with certain works of Tallis, Byrd and Gibbons, was by no means neglected.

JOHN GOSS (1800–80) was a chorister in the Chapel Royal and afterwards became a pupil of Attwood, whom he succeeded as organist of St Paul's Cathedral in 1838. He was knighted in 1872 after the Thanksgiving Service for the recovery of the Prince of Wales (later Edward VII). In this same year he resigned his post at St Paul's.

It cannot be said that his church music displays exceptional talent; but it is sincere and effective for its purpose, and it is well written for the voices – a quality that has enabled it to retain a large place in the cathedral repertory in more recent times. His output of anthems was large, though his work was very uneven. He understood the cathedral style of anthem, and he reached a fair standard of excellence in such work as *The Wilderness*, which is perhaps the best of his longer anthems. The second recitative of this anthem ends beautifully with the phrase 'but the redeemed shall walk there'; the sustained high

D admirably produces a feeling of repose and security. *Lord, let me know mine end* was originally composed for different words on the occasion of the annual Festival of the Sons of the Clergy in St Paul's Cathedral. The substitution of words of quite another character inevitably detracts from its artistic value, but the concluding passage is effective. *Praise the Lord, O my soul* and *O taste and see*, which formerly enjoyed wide popularity, hardly rise above the commonplace; and there are several others that have little to commend them, although they seldom fall below the level of respectable mediocrity. On the other hand *Lift up thine eyes* deserves a high place in cathedral music. The opening chorus of this anthem for double choir is a fine bit of writing. Four short anthems by this composer are first-rate: *O saviour of the world*, *If we believe*, *Almighty and everlasting God*, and *God so loved the world*. The last, hardly more than a miniature, is admirably fitted to the words and perfectly phrased. *O saviour of the world* begins quietly, and as it gradually increases in force, a triumphant climax is reached at the words 'hast redeemed us'. This adds much to the beauty of the rest of the prayer, expressed in soft phrases which repeat the opening melody:

Goss's Evening Service in E major is an excellent example of the Short Service in its nineteenth-century dress. It can be sung without accompaniment.

SAMUEL SEBASTIAN WESLEY (1810–76) was the illegitimate son of Samuel Wesley. He began his career as a chorister in the Chapel Royal, and at the age of 22 became organist of Hereford Cathedral, moving in 1835 to Exeter Cathedral. It was during his six years at Exeter that he earned the position of the foremost composer of English cathedral music as well as the best executant on the organ. In 1842 he left Exeter for Leeds Parish Church, having in the meanwhile taken the Oxford degree of D.Mus. It was at this period that Spohr wrote of him that 'he is master of both style and form . . . his sacred music is chiefly distinguished by a noble, often even an antique style, and by rich harmonies as well as by surprisingly beautiful modulations'. In 1849 he was appointed organist of Winchester Cathedral and also of the College. The last of his many moves was made in 1865 when he left Winchester for Gloucester Cathedral, where he remained till his death. He was buried at Exeter. Apart from his compositions he was an enthusiast on the subject of cathedrals and cathedral music. He wrote more than one pamphlet deploring the low standard to which the performance of the music had fallen, and he had hard words to say about the indifference shown by some of the capitular bodies in their attitude towards the musical services. He also expressed regret that the singers were so few in number in many of the cathedral choirs, and held strong views on the desirability of reforming the cathedral system.

Two characteristic features of his longer anthems are the recitatives and the arias. The recitatives have a very individual character and are unlike anything else in English cathedral music. They are very definitely English in style, and the accentuation and phrasing are those of a musician with a literary background. The arias are similar in scope and purpose to those of Handel and Bach. They are remarkable for their melodic beauty as well as for their dramatic features, many of the effects being secured by bold modulations. They show a great advance on anything of the kind previously found in cathedral music, notably when compared with the verse solos in Greene's anthems. Examples are 'Thou, O Lord God' from *Let us lift up our heart*; 'Who can express?' from *O give thanks*; 'Say to them' from *The wilderness*; and 'Our heart shall rejoice' from *O Lord, thou art my God*.

The wilderness was written before Goss's setting of the same text. A comparison of the two works serves to show at once the superiority of Wesley's imaginative gifts, as well as his technical resources as a musician. The harmonic clashes resulting from the use of sequence in the following passage suggest that, like his father, he had learned something from Bach's polyphony:

A magnificent climax to the exuberant chorus 'And the ransomed of the Lord' is produced by a succession of striking modulations. Thus, after the very florid passages in which all the voices join, the thought of the final return of the exiles is gloriously expressed in the following bars in which the emphasis on the word 'return' must be specially noticed; the effect is much enhanced by the series of modulations:

The *fortissimo* is sustained to the very end. This may be one of the passages which Wesley had in his mind when he expressed the opinion that the number of men in cathedral choirs was inadequate. The section with which this anthem ends has been thought by some to be too sentimental. Others have criticized the chromatic harmonies in it as reminiscent of Spohr. The first point is a matter of opinion; the second point cannot be supported in the light of a careful comparison with Spohr's idiom.

Ascribe unto the Lord opens with recitative in Wesley's characteristic manner, sung in unison by all the men's voices. The touch of a master craftsman is shown in the repetition of the passage 'Let the whole earth stand in awe of him' after the second recitative. It is to be sung the first time with full strength, expressing adoration, but the second time *pianissimo* in hushed awe before the presence of God. This fine anthem must be passed by with no more than a mention of the flowing melodiousness of the final chorus, and a warning that the chorus 'As for the gods of the heathen' is marked *Allegretto* by the composer, who designed it in a mocking spirit.

Blessed be the God and Father was originally composed for Easter Day at Hereford Cathedral on an occasion when only trebles and a single bass were available. It was subsequently revised and published in its present form. It begins with a kind of unaccompanied choral recitative, beginning softly and building up an effective climax, reinforced by the organ at the words 'the resurrection of Jesus Christ from the dead'. The strength of the final chord gains much by the basses rising to the high E♭. The recitative is continued by the men's voices in unison and carried still further in a passage for treble solo, which is in the nature of mensurate recitative, the words being sung straight through without repetition. There is further recitative for men's voices at the words 'Being born again' before the final chorus with its dramatic opening.

Let us lift up our heart is of great length and cannot well be performed in its entirety at the ordinary cathedral service. The bass solo in this anthem, already mentioned, is the finest of all Wesley's arias, beautiful in its expression of the spirit of intimate prayer. The first section of this song, which begins in B minor, ends reposefully after the fervent appeal 'haste thee to help me':

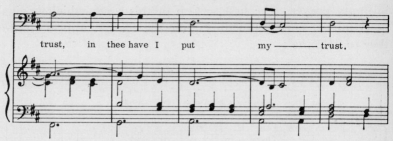

The reiteration of the first subject follows in B minor as before;
and as the strong feeling of fervour revives again with the
words 'haste thee to help me', the first subject is brought in
with thrilling effect in C major:

The aria ends with increasing fervour expressed in sudden changes of key and in a wide use of the compass of the bass voice.

This anthem begins with a double chorus, developed at considerable length. It contains some fine part-writing, but the latter part of it is mainly for four voices only. Then follows a rather curious section beginning with the words 'Be not very sore'. It is nominally for a quartet of voices, but in the first instance the phrases are assigned to each voice singly in turn; the voices first combine at the words 'See, we beseech thee' and the full choir joins in alternate phrases. This section is not of the same high quality as the rest of the anthem. After the bass aria comes a setting of Charles Wesley's hymn *Thou judge of quick and dead*, and the anthem ends with a fugal chorus to the words 'O may we thus insure a lot among the blest'.

O Lord, thou art my God is a little longer still, and for the same reason it is not widely known or performed. There are some who consider it to be Wesley's finest work. The anthem includes choruses for double choir and for five voices. It contains some especially fine moments: one of these is when all the voices break into unison at the words 'for the Lord hath spoken it', and again, at the climax towards the end, at the words 'Lo, this is the Lord'.

The face of the Lord is chiefly remarkable for the bold handling of the phrase 'the righteous cry' towards the end of the double quartet (shown overleaf).

Other fine anthems on the big scale are *Praise the Lord* and *O give thanks*. Among the shorter anthems *Cast me not away*, for six voices, is outstanding. It is said to have been written when the composer was suffering from a broken arm. *Thou wilt keep him*, beautiful as it is, is a little spoilt by the passage 'for thine is the kingdom', which is rather out of character with the rest of the anthem. *Wash me throughly* and *O Lord my God* are exquisite examples of Wesley's sincere and reverent treatment of short prayers of a penitential character. *Man that is born of a woman* is noteworthy for the beauty of the closing bars, and the expressive discords at the word 'bitter':

These three sentences were expressly composed by Wesley to precede Purcell's setting of the final sentence, *Thou knowest, Lord*.

Wesley's Service in E major marks very great progress in the development of this particular class of composition. Nothing so elaborate in design had previously been attempted for ordinary daily use. It is perhaps a little disjointed, but there is variety and much good music in both the Morning and Evening sections, and it includes a fine setting of the *Credo*. The Short Service in F major and the chant Service are established items in the cathedral repertory.

THOMAS ATTWOOD WALMISLEY (1814–56) was the son of Thomas Forbes Walmisley, a musician whose interest turned to the composition of glees and other secular music rather than to church music, though his Service in C major was at one time performed in several cathedrals. The younger Walmisley was a godson of Attwood and became his pupil. In 1833 he became organist of Trinity and St John's Colleges, Cambridge, and three years later succeeded Clarke-Whitfeld as Professor of Music in the University. His father survived him for ten years and edited his volume of cathedral music. Walmisley was a musician of wide culture and interests. He was a good mathematician and lecturer, and one of the first Englishmen to recognize Bach's B minor Mass as 'the greatest composition in the world'.

His finest composition for cathedral use is his Evening Service in D minor. He shares with Wesley the distinction of raising the character and design of the service from the dull stereotyped form into which it had sunk in the eighteenth century. The D minor Service is the earliest work of the kind in which the organ plays an important and prominent part; yet it never displaces or supersedes the voices in their primary purpose. In the concluding passage of the *Gloria* of both canticles Walmisley has worked upon a fine bass phrase borrowed from works by Henri Dumont, a Belgian priest-organist in the seventeenth century. This was no plagiarism; the source of the bass was acknowledged in the printed editions of the Service. Walmisley's Full Service in D major can be sung without accompaniment; it is rather an uneven work, some of the phrases in *Te Deum* being unduly cramped. The modulation to B♭ in *Magnificat* was a favourite device of Walmisley's. It is found again, for instance, near the end of the short anthem or 'choral hymn', as he calls it, *From all that dwell*, where the modulation is from F major to D♭ major. The B♭ major Evening Service is an impressive work in eight parts. The Morning Service in B♭ major, in four parts, is a simpler work and does not actually belong to the big Evening Service. Walmisley also wrote a Full Service in F major with *Cantate* and *Deus misereatur*, and another straightforward setting for four voices in C major.

His anthems are on the whole disappointing. The best of them is *Hear, O thou shepherd of Israel*, particularly the quiet chorus 'Turn us again', the alto recitative and aria, and the beautiful little choral passage that intervenes with the words 'How long wilt thou be angry?' *If the Lord himself had not been on our side* was written as a special thanksgiving anthem. It is rather a noisy and pretentious work with a very prominent organ part: the treble solo 'Our soul is escaped' is trivial and the chorus that follows it is made up of the same melodic material. The final chorus is reminiscent of the so-called 'Hallelujah' chorus in Beethoven's *Christus am Ölberg*. Among the less known of the anthems is *O give thanks*, written for a commemoration at Trinity College, Cambridge. Like so many of Walmisley's anthems, it is uneven in interest, but the choral writing is effective, particularly the final chorus for double choir.

JOHN BACCHUS DYKES (1823–76) was a pupil of Walmisley at Cambridge. He was ordained in 1847 and became precentor of Durham. He is best known by his hymn-tunes, but his Service in F major and his anthem for All Saints' Day, *These are they*, retained their popularity until the end of the nineteenth century.

FREDERICK ARTHUR GORE OUSELEY (1825–89) began his career as an infant prodigy. His parents, both of them people of wide culture, were well-known personalities in London Society when, at a very early age, the exceptional musical gifts of the child first revealed themselves. The prejudices of the time, however, precluded the idea of his becoming a professional musician, since he was the heir to his father's baronetcy and property. He would certainly become a great amateur of music, but his education must follow conventional lines; he must go in due course to Oxford and be ordained. Consequently as a child he received little strict musical training, let alone the intensive course which should have been his due. As a child he displayed romantic feeling in his compositions; by the time he matriculated at Christ Church romance had practically been destroyed for him by the course of a Latin and Greek education which he consistently disliked. Once his father saw him in a rage, stamping on his Greek play. 'It's no good, Frederick,' he said, 'you've got to do it.' Gaisford, Dean of Christ Church, told Ouseley, when he proposed to take the

B.Mus. degree, that it was unbecoming for a man in his position to present himself for examination in music in the University.[1]

Ouseley composed an immense amount of church music – as many as eleven services and about 70 anthems. Very few of these can be described as anything but academic. An exception is *O Saviour of the world*, a short unaccompanied work of great beauty for double choir. *From the rising of the sun*, *Is it nothing to you?* and *How goodly are thy tents* are also excellent little pieces in the true cathedral style.

Ouseley made three valuable contributions to cathedral music. First, in the foundation and endowment of St Michael's College, Tenbury, for the purpose of maintaining daily choral services on cathedral lines, regardless of what might happen to the cathedrals themselves in the event of disestablishment and disendowment, which he regarded as imminent in his own time. Secondly, as a musicologist. In this field he did a large amount of original research, making a special study of sixteenth-century church music and scoring a great number of the services and anthems of that period. Thirdly, in collecting a music library which now takes a place among the most important in Europe.

Besides being Warden of his own college and vicar of St Michael's parish, Ouseley was precentor of Hereford Cathedral and Professor of Music at Oxford University.

HENRY THOMAS SMART (1813–79) was a nephew of Sir George Smart, who was a notable personality in musical circles during a very long life, particularly as a conductor. Henry Smart's church music, once familiar in cathedral services, is now completely forgotten. Like many other Victorian composers he fell into the error of attaching to the instrumental ideals of rhythm and form greater importance than to those of verbal phrasing and accentuation, sometimes sacrificing the latter to the former. His Service in F major, especially, is in almost perpetual bondage to this system, some verses being expanded and others compressed so that each succeeding period of eight bars may be undisturbed in its regularity and subdivided with equal regularity into two sections of four bars

[1] J. S. Bumpus, *A History of English Cathedral Music*, p. 536.

each, with a halt every four bars. Among his anthems *The Lord hath done great things*, *O God, the king of glory* and *Sing unto the Lord* enjoyed popularity until the end of the nineteenth century.

WILLIAM STERNDALE BENNETT (1816–75) was a chorister at King's College, Cambridge, with an exceptionally beautiful voice. He received his musical training under Crotch and Cipriani Potter as a scholar of the Royal Academy of Music. At this period he was brought to the notice of Mendelssohn, who was present at Bennett's performance of his own pianoforte concerto in D minor. Subsequently he went to Leipzig and was introduced by Mendelssohn to Robert Schumann, who received him with enthusiasm and wrote of him in terms of the highest praise. Later in life he became Professor of Music at Cambridge, and he was also Principal of the Royal Academy of Music. He is one of the few Englishmen to have earned recognition on the Continent; in 1853 he was offered, but refused, the conductorship of the Gewandhaus concerts in Leipzig. In the following year he directed the first performance in England of Bach's *St. Matthew Passion*, and in 1856 he was appointed conductor of the Philharmonic Society. He was knighted in 1871.

Bennett wrote some excellent works for orchestra and the pianoforte but little for the Church. Mention should be made, however, of his eight-part motet *In thee, O Lord*, which is superior to the rest of his slender output in this field.

ROBERT LUCAS PEARSALL (1795–1856) was a barrister by profession, but his heart was entirely in music. He is best known for his madrigalian part-songs, but his anthems are now almost entirely forgotten, although a whole volume of them together with a setting of the Lord's Prayer was published. His name, however, is kept alive by his admirable arrangement of the carol *In dulci jubilo*.

GEORGE JOB ELVEY (1816–93) became organist of St George's Chapel, Windsor, at the early age of 19. During his long tenure of office he wrote a large amount of cathedral music, much of which enjoyed great popularity until the end of the nineteenth century. Little of it has sufficient inspiration to enable it to endure the test of time.

JAMES TURLE (1802–82) was organist of Westminster Abbey from 1831 to 1875. Apart from his chants his only other contribution of any consequence to cathedral music is his Service in D major, which can be sung effectively without accompaniment.

GEORGE ALEXANDER MACFARREN (1813–87) wrote a large number of instrumental and vocal works, including operas, symphonies and oratorios. He succeeded Sterndale Bennett as Professor of Music at Cambridge, and as Principal of the Royal Academy of Music. A Service in E major and a short anthem, *The Lord is my shepherd*, may be mentioned among the few pieces of church music written by him.

EDWIN GEORGE MONK (1819–1900), a pupil of Macfarren, became organist of York Minster in 1859. He took a special interest in Anglican chanting and was associated with Ouseley in producing *The Psalter and Canticles pointed for chanting*.

WILLIAM HENRY MONK (1823–89), apparently no relation, was chiefly interested in hymnology. He was one of the music editors of *Hymns Ancient and Modern*.

CHAPTER 18

Mid-Victorian Composers

In an illuminating little treatise[1] Sir Henry Hadow stated that there are 'three diseases from which religious music can suffer: the disease of virtuosity, which over-elaborates the technique of composition and so tends to lose sight of its meaning; the disease of theatricalism, which over-emphasizes the meaning at the expense of true dignity and reverence; and the disease of sentimentalism, which enervates the meaning by relaxing it into a soft and facile prettiness'. It was this third disease which in his opinion attacked the English composers of the mid-Victorian period, prominent among whom were Garrett, Barnby, Stainer and Sullivan, to name them in order of seniority although there was no more than eight years between them in age. These composers came under entirely new influences; and the change of style, especially in their anthems, is to be accounted for in various directions. The dominating influence came from abroad, and from the works of three composers in particular – Spohr, Mendelssohn and Gounod. It is not easy at this distance of time to recapture the overwhelming admiration and enthusiasm with which the works of these composers were received in England, nor the extent to which they influenced English musicians, both professional and amateur, in their own time and for a generation or two later.

Mendelssohn was already a popular hero in London before *Elijah* was produced at the Birmingham Festival in 1846. His position withstood criticism for at least another 50 or 60 years, after which his reputation suffered, by contrast, too severe a depreciation. His influence was felt by cathedral musicians in

[1] *Church Music* (London, 1926).

two directions. First, composers adopted his methods and style as their model, which they followed from afar off. Secondly, a number of excerpts from *Elijah*, *St. Paul* and other sacred works came into frequent use as anthems.

Spohr was an older man, but late in his life and at this same period he earned the admiration of English people to an extent which was far out of proportion to his actual worth as a composer. His influence also on cathedral music was considerable. His harmonic idiom was seductive, and composers fell under the spell of his sensuous use of chromatic chords and modulations. His works were also drawn upon largely for use as anthems. Excerpts from *The Last Judgement* loomed large in cathedral lists throughout the rest of the century, and trivialities such as his *As pants the hart* were extremely popular.

Gounod was younger than Spohr and Mendelssohn, but his influence began to be felt soon after the production of his *Messe solennelle* in London in 1851. His music appealed to English church people at that time, all the more strongly because he was a man of deep religious convictions and at one time had contemplated ordination. He spent many years in this country and was the founder of the Royal Choral Society, first called the Albert Hall Choral Society. At this time he wrote English anthems of the emotional type that especially appealed to English churchgoers. Cathedral music was less affected by his influence than by Mendelssohn's, apart from the actual inclusion of many of his anthems. The compositions belonging to this group were characterized rather by that form of sentimentalism, which, as Hadow remarked, 'enervates the meaning by relaxing it into a soft and easy prettiness'. It was futility and poverty of idea rather than sentiment that resulted in so many empty and meaningless phrases. There was another influence at work, namely that of the part-song. This form of composition was comparatively a novelty at this date, and it owed its popularity in England largely to Henry Smart. Many of the anthems of the mid-Victorian period were designed very much on the lines of accompanied part-songs, if allowance is made for the difference between setting poetry and prose.

JOHN STAINER (1840–1901) was undoubtedly the most

distinguished of this group of cathedral musicians. He began his career as a chorister at St Paul's Cathedral, where his exceptional gifts were quickly recognized and developed. In 1856 he became the first organist of St Michael's College, Tenbury, and in 1859 organist of Magdalen College, Oxford. He left Oxford for St Paul's Cathedral in 1872 and was knighted on his retirement in 1888. He succeeded Ouseley as Professor of Music at Oxford in 1889. He excelled in many branches of his art. He was a fine organist with exceptional skill in *extempore* playing. One of the ablest choir-trainers of his generation, he succeeded in the arduous task of making the choir of St Paul's Cathedral the best in England, though he took it over in a wretched state of disorganization; and as a pioneer he did a great work in creating there a standard for the choral celebration of the Holy Communion service. He was an excellent lecturer, and he did much to raise the status of the Professorship of Music at Oxford while he held the chair. He also did much valuable work in the field of musicology.

Almost all Stainer's anthems suffer primarily from a failure to match with music the magnificence of his verbal texts. This is all the more noticeable since he selected for many of them some of the finest passages in the Bible. Whereas so many composers have looked mainly to the Psalms, Stainer chose texts from Isaiah several times, from Ecclesiasticus, from the Book of Wisdom, Ezekiel, Zechariah, Baruch and Job, as well as from the Revelation and various Epistles of St Paul; only a few of his anthems are from the Psalms. In this matter he showed a commendable originality and at the same time fine literary sense, but set himself a task which proved far too severe for him. It may be wondered whether he realized this. He did in fact know that he had written most of his earlier anthems too easily. Within a year of his death he expressed his regret that so many of them had been published, adding that they had been written in response to pressure put upon him in early days by the clergy and others, who assured him that they were 'just the thing they wanted'. Hadow was right when he said[1] that 'this music was deplorably easy to write'. Beautiful language has a very definite value and share in making for the success of any piece of vocal music, and it is possible that the

[1] *Op. cit.*, p. 24.

popularity of many of Stainer's anthems may at least in part be explained by his fine taste in the choice of words.

Stainer's 'part-song' manner is exemplified by his setting of glorious words from the Book of Job in *The morning stars sang together*, which begins:

And one cannot help feeling that the following passage from
What are these? is inadequate as an expression of the words:

On the other hand in *I saw the Lord* there is a certain dignity in
the opening movement, a double chorus in eight parts, and
some attempt at realism in the description of how 'the posts
of the door were moved', 'and the house was filled with smoke'.
It is unfortunate that the melodic material of the last movement, 'O Trinity, O Unity', should not be more in keeping
with the solemnity of the words, but much ingenuity is shown
in the combination of the *Ter sanctus* with the main melody by
skilful eight-part writing.

It is worth nothing that the mid-Victorian composers were
the first to make a general practice of including *Sanctus* and
Gloria in excelsis in their full services; but it was exceptional at
this time to find settings of *Cantate* and *Deus misereatur*. The best
of Stainer's full services is that in E♭ major; but all of them are
of greater musical interest than his anthems. The B♭ major
Service was written with special reference to the acoustic conditions of St Paul's Cathedral. It sounds ineffective in most
other buildings; and to begin a phrase with good tone on a high
B♭, as in the *Gloria* of the Evening Service, is beyond the capa-

bility of most choristers. Stainer had known St Paul's and its peculiar acoustic properties from his chorister days onwards; and they exercised a very definite influence upon his compositions. The same thing is indeed true to some extent of all cathedral composers. Nor are the varied acoustic conditions the only influences which may make for individual characteristics in composition. The influence of particular singers, such as John Gostling, in Purcell's time, has already been mentioned.[1] In more modern times S. S. Wesley had in mind a splendid bass lay-clerk at Winchester Cathedral named Penuel Cross for some of the solos in his anthems. Cross was appointed in 1847, two years before Wesley came to Winchester, and retired in 1890. The influence of the organ as an instrument for accompanying the choir must also be considered, especially in relation to its development from the time of Father Smith to Father Willis, that is to say from Purcell to Stanford. The invention of the swell and the tardy arrival in England of the full pedal-board are among important developments which have influenced the style of writing organ accompaniments.

JOSEPH BARNBY (1838–96) was one of a large family; several of his brothers, like him, became choristers of York Minster and followed music as their profession. While organist of St Anne's, Soho, he made it an annual custom to perform Bach's *St. John Passion* with full orchestra, and in 1871 he conducted one of the early performances in England of the *St. Matthew Passion*. He was in fact an enthusiast for Bach's music when it was little known in England. He was also a first-rate choirmaster; he was closely associated with Gounod in forming the Albert Hall Choral Society and succeeded him as its conductor. He served as precentor of Eton College from 1875 to 1892 and became Principal of the Guildhall School of Music in the latter year, when he was knighted. It is unfortunate that his gifts as a composer, whether of anthems or part-songs, were not commensurate with the services he rendered in the field of performance.

GEORGE MURSELL GARRETT (1834–97) was a chorister at New College, Oxford, under Stephen Elvey, and from 1857

[1] pp. 133 and 165.

onwards was organist of St John's College, Cambridge. He made his reputation mainly as a composer of services. The foundation of the modern cathedral service had actually been laid by T. A. Walmisley and Sebastian Wesley; but Garrett, who was a pupil of Wesley, was one of the first to develop the organ-part as an independent feature of the composition, making it contribute something of positive value which could not be supplied by the voices alone. Smart, Stainer, Barnby and many others followed quickly on the same lines. Garrett's full services in D major and F major held their place in the repertory more successfully than those of other mid-Victorian composers.

ARTHUR SEYMOUR SULLIVAN (1842–1900) was a composer of outstanding gifts. In early life he was closely associated with church music. He entered the Chapel Royal as a chorister in 1854, and his first anthem was written while he was still there. At the Royal Academy of Music he was a pupil of Sterndale Bennett and Goss. In 1856 he was the first to be awarded the Mendelssohn Scholarship, which made possible further study at Leipzig. In 1861 he was appointed organist of St Michael's, Chester Square, a position which he held for several years together with a similar appointment at St Peter's, Cranley Gardens.

His contributions to church music suggest that, in spite of his remarkable facility, he was not vitally interested in it. Too often the idiom of his anthems is out of keeping with the splendour of the words. The following example seems curiously akin to Jack Point's music in *The Yeomen of the Guard*:

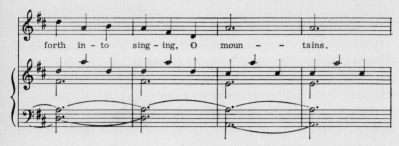

forth in-to sing-ing, O moun - - tains.

CHARLES STEGGALL (1826–1905) became organist of Lincoln's Inn Chapel in 1864 and was one of the founders of the Royal College of Organists in that year. His anthem *God came from Teman* suffers from the inadequacy of the treatment of the words. The composer seems to have completely misunderstood the imaginative text from Habakkuk. *Remember now thy Creator* is a far better work; the movement beginning 'While the sun, or the light, or the moon, or the stars, be not darkened' is handled with much poetic feeling and mystery.

Other composers belonging to this period can be dismissed with a few words; none of them have contributed anything to the repertory that is likely to retain its place. HERBERT STANLEY OAKELEY (1830–1903), Professor of Music at Edinburgh from 1865, is remembered by his quadruple chant and some hymn-tunes. PHILIP ARMES (1836–1908) became organist of Durham Cathedral in 1862, having previously held a similar position at Chichester for a year. His anthem *Give ear, O ye heavens* had a considerable measure of popularity in Victorian days. BERTHOLD TOURS (1838–97), a Netherlander by birth, lived in England from 1861 and became musical adviser to the firm of Novello. This connexion brought him into close touch with English cathedral music for many years, and a large number of his hymn-tunes, anthems and services became popular, though without any substantial justification.

CHAPTER 19

Late Victorian and Edwardian Composers

The present chapter is designed roughly to cover the last decade of the nineteenth century and the first decade of the twentieth. The last fifteen years of the nineteenth century were marked by a very notable revival of British music, though its effect upon church music was to be still further delayed. In Hadow's opinion[1] it originated in the production of Hubert Parry's choral ode *Promethus Unbound* at the Gloucester Festival in 1880. It may be that, in his enthusiastic admiration for Parry's work, he somewhat overstated the importance of this particular composition and the occasion of its first performance. Nevertheless, it is undeniable that during the ten years or so that followed the musical taste of the British people, composers and listeners alike, showed a remarkable improvement.

Among the composers Alexander Mackenzie, Hubert Parry and Charles Stanford were especially prominent as leaders of this renaissance. The three were much of an age, born respectively in 1847, 1848 and 1852. In the early nineties they were in the prime of life and in the full vigour of their musical achievements. Apart from their important spheres of influence in the teaching branch of their profession, each of them by this time had produced a number of compositions markedly superior to anything written by their immediate predecessors – operas, oratorios, symphonies, concertos and chamber music. Of these three composers, however, only Stanford has an important place in cathedral music. Mackenzie, apart from a few early anthems, wrote nothing, and Parry's contribution was small.

Before discussing Stanford it will be convenient to deal with some of the lesser men, such as J. F. Bridge, G. C. Martin and

[1] *Collected Essays*, p. 149.

J. V. Roberts. These were younger than the composers discussed in the previous chapter, but the character of their church music shows little or no advance upon that of a generation earlier, though they all survived the outbreak of the 1914–18 War.

JOHN FREDERICK BRIDGE (1844–1924) began his career as a chorister of Rochester Cathedral. In 1869 he was appointed organist of Manchester Cathedral, and six years later became organist of Westminster Abbey. In this position, which he held for 36 years, he was responsible for the music of the ceremonial services at the Abbey on the occasion of Queen Victoria's Jubilee in 1887 and the coronations of Edward VII and George V. He was knighted in 1897. His cathedral music is very disappointing, for his gifts and academic skill gave promise of something far better. His anthems suffer from a lack of seriousness and a failure to appreciate the responsibilities inseparable from setting to music the great literature of the Bible and Prayer Book.

GEORGE CLEMENT MARTIN (1844–1916) was organist of St Paul's Cathedral from 1888 until his death. He was knighted on the occasion of Queen Victoria's Diamond Jubilee in 1897, having composed a special *Te Deum* for the ceremonial service held on the steps outside the West door of St Paul's. He wrote as many as six services, those in C major and A major being in wide use during his lifetime, as well as a number of anthems. The sentimentality of his music, however, has been fatal to its survival.

JOHN VARLEY ROBERTS (1841–1920) was organist of Magdalen College, Oxford, where he trained the choir with remarkable efficiency for 37 years, from 1882 to 1919. As a composer he remained faithful throughout his career to the mid-Victorian school and its influences. His output of church music included five services and about 50 anthems, many of which gained great popularity, especially in his native county of Yorkshire; but it has since shared the fate of almost all the cathedral music of this character.

CHARLES HARFORD LLOYD (1849–1919) was successively organist of Gloucester Cathedral and Christ Church, Oxford,

and precentor of Eton College from 1892 to 1914. He is best
known by his full service (including the Communion Office)
in E♭ major, but his unaccompanied anthem, *The righteous live
for evermore*, the opening movement of a longer work, is a far
better work and an admirable example of eight-part writing.

It is a relief, on the whole, to turn to the music of CHARLES
VILLIERS STANFORD (1852–1924). He was born in Dublin
and in early days was a pupil of Robert Stewart. He went up to
Cambridge with an organ scholarship at Queen's College, and
a classical scholarship was soon added. While still an undergraduate he was appointed organist of Trinity College in 1873.
He was given the D.Mus. degree at Oxford in 1883 and the
Mus.D. at Cambridge in 1888. In 1887 he succeeded Macfarren
as Professor of Music at Cambridge. At the Royal College of
Music he exerted a very wide and important influence upon a
series of distinguished pupils as a teacher of composition. He
was knighted in 1901.

As many as five of Stanford's services are in general use.
In addition to these is his service on plainsong tones. In this
particular class of composition he set up a new standard of
design and character. His method in setting the canticles has
been described as 'symphonic'. This may be taken to mean that
each canticle was designed in a more coherent manner than
formerly. Previously composers had worked on what has been
called a 'point-to-point' method, treating each section in succession in accordance with its particular requirements without any special regard to other sections. Stanford welded his
settings into one whole, not only by means of well-designed
successions of modulation and with a fine sense of proportion
in planning his climaxes, but also by the use of melodic figures
or motives, which by their recurrence bind the work together
and give it continuity. Many of these were taken from plainsong sources. For instance, in the B♭ major Service, an early
work, the composer states that he 'has (in the *Te Deum*, *Credo*
and *Gloria in excelsis*) made use of Gregorian Intonations, as
well as of the *Amen* according to the Dresden use'. The following
example, where the intonation is incorporated in the organ part,
is from the *Creed*:

The opening phrase of the B♭ major *Magnificat* provides a good example of Stanford's care for accentuation. The drop of a fifth gives perfect emphasis to the word 'magnify':

The A major Evening Service followed soon after the B♭ major. It was originally composed with orchestral accompaniment for the Festival of the Sons of the Clergy in 1880. The morning canticles and Communion Service were added in 1895. In the *Te Deum* Stanford shows considerable dramatic power in expressing the majesty of the three persons of the Trinity. Each of the three phrases begins with the unaccompanied voices in unison; and the six-part chord, suddenly reinforced by the organ, is extremely telling. The three persons are equally acclaimed in the same musical phrase and with equal power. The dignified *Gloria Patri* for double choir is identical in all the canticles of this service; and here too the three persons of the Trinity are represented each with the same musical phrase. In the *Nunc Dimittis* the first words of the canticle are sung again just before the *Gloria Patri*. Effective though this is, it is questionable whether it is appropriate in a canticle which is part of the Office of Evensong.

The F major Service is simpler in character and is effective when sung without accompaniment, with the exception of *Benedictus qui venit* and *Agnus Dei*, which do not actually belong to this service, having been designed for use with either the F major, the B♭ major, the A major or the C major. The G major Service, published in 1904, is rather lighter in character than the rest. In the *Magnificat* Stanford had the idea in his mind that, in accordance with Jewish custom at the period, the Virgin might have been little more than a child at the time of the birth of Christ; so he pictured her with a spinning-wheel happily singing *Magnificat*. It is consequently scored for treble solo with choral and organ accompaniment and a spinning-wheel obbligato for a flute stop.

The 'Evening Service on the 2nd and 3rd tones' is of an experimental character. The plainsong is sung in unison in alternate verses, answered by the voices in four-part harmony with a very free treatment of the plainsong melodies. The experiment is not entirely successful, for the fundamental differences between the two methods are in a sense irreconcilable under such a scheme as this. Nevertheless, Stanford's rare technical skill, coupled with his gift for thematic phrasing, has given a quality to this service which makes it welcome as an occasional contrast to more conventional compositions. Stanford himself regarded his Service in C major, published in 1909, as his best.

Stanford composed a large number of anthems, almost all of which are distinguished by first-rate craftsmanship and sincerity of purpose. The early *The Lord is my shepherd* is one of the most effective. *If ye then be risen with Christ*, also written before the end of the nineteenth century, is founded upon the theme of the *Alleluia* in the Easter hymn *Jesus Christ is risen to-day*, known as 'Salisbury'. In the introductory bars it is partially disguised by the addition of three crotchets leading into it and by the lengthening of the last notes of the phrase. In the second movement it appears in shorter notes cutting across two bars of triple time. Finally in a contrapuntal movement it emerges brilliantly in its original shape in the high register of the treble voices. At a later date Stanford produced a set of three motets with English words, Op. 135: *Ye holy angels bright* for eight voices, *Eternal Father* for six, and *Glorious and powerful God* for four. The last of his anthems was *Lo, I raise up that bitter and hasty nation*, written during the 1914–18 War – a dramatic and forceful work. It ends with the assurance that the fury and terrors of war will pass, and 'the earth shall be filled with the knowledge of the glory of the Lord as the waters cover the sea'.

CHARLES HUBERT HASTINGS PARRY (1848–1918) showed promise at an early age. He took the B.Mus. degree before leaving Eton for Exeter College, Oxford. He studied under Sterndale Bennett and G. A. Macfarren, and later at Stuttgart under Hugo Pierson, but it was not for some time after going down from Oxford that he made music his profession. He was appointed Director of the Royal College of Music in 1894 and was Professor of Music at Oxford, in succession to Stainer, from 1900 to 1908. He received honorary doctorates from Oxford, Cambridge and Dublin, was knighted in 1898 and created a baronet in 1902. His interests lay mainly outside church music, but he wrote two very fine anthems. *I was glad* was composed for the coronation of Edward VII. As a piece of occasional music it could scarcely be improved upon. It seizes on the excitement that culminates at the moment when the sovereign enters the Abbey and is acclaimed with the shouts of 'Vivat!' The middle movement, 'O pray for the peace of Jerusalem', is beautiful in its quiet contrast to the opening, and the final movement ends with great dignity in the combined strength of the full chorus and orchestra. The other anthem, *Hear my words, O my people*, is laid out on a grand scale in the tradition of Boyce and Wesley. The first chorus is followed by a bass solo, which ends with a very characteristic phrase:

The semi-chorus, or quartet, 'Behold the eye of the Lord', makes an effective contrast after the stately proclamation by the full choir 'The Lord's seat is in Heaven'. The final chorus takes the form of a hymn-tune to the words 'O praise ye the Lord', which is worked up to a telling climax before the final *Amen.* The *Songs of Farewell* do not properly rank as anthems, with the exception of *Lord, let me know mine end,* which is an impressive unaccompanied motet for double choir. To be really effective this work needs to be performed by a larger body than the ordinary cathedral choir. The second bass voice has several sustained passages in a very low register, and these must sound thin if no more than a single voice is employed.

ALAN GRAY (1855–1935) originally intended, as an undergraduate at Trinity College, Cambridge, to make the law his profession. Subsequently he studied music under E. G. Monk of York Minster, and took the degrees of Mus.B. and Mus.D. He became Director of Music at Wellington College in 1883 and succeeded Stanford as organist of Trinity College in 1892.

He wrote as many as six services. The *Te Deum* of the G major Service is designed to observe the original structure of the hymn, ending with the words 'in glory everlasting'. Gray in his preface, quoting Dean Burn, uses the expression 'subsequent additions' in reference to the final eight verses. This may convey a misleading impression. These 'subsequent additions' were made probably no more than a century later than the rest of the hymn, which dates from the beginning of the fifth century, and the musical settings, both Latin and English, have now for many centuries treated the 'additions' as an integral part of the whole. To break off at this point and to set the 'additions' as versicles must be regarded as unnecessary pedantry, and the musical effect is most unsatisfactory. Gray also wrote an Evening Service in F minor for double choir, in the *Magnificat* of which he makes the mistake of repeating the word 'holy' three times in the sentence 'and holy is his Name', under the erroneous impression that it has some allusion to the *Sanctus* of the Communion Office and to the *Ter sanctus* in *Te Deum*. His anthem *What are these that glow from afar?*, published in 1928, is a much later work.

BASIL HARWOOD (1859–1949) was organist of Ely Cathedral from 1887 to 1892 and subsequently of Christ Church, Oxford, until 1909, when he retired. The rest of his life was spent without any professional appointment, though he continued to compose. He wrote a considerable amount of church music; but on the whole his music for the choir, apart from the anthem *O how glorious is the kingdom*, made less impact than his organ music, which was inventive, though not always disciplined, and effectively written for the type of instrument to which he was accustomed.

CHARLES WOOD (1866–1926) was for many years organist of Gonville and Caius College, Cambridge, and Professor of Music, in succession to Stanford, for the last two years of his life. He was a prolific composer, faithful to tradition in the face of experiment but in no way a reactionary; even his early services, especially the Communion Service in the Phrygian mode, are evidence of that, for here he was adapting old forms to modern uses. Some of his methods were new and original – for example, the employment of a French melody as the foundation upon which his eight-part *Nunc dimittis* in F major is constructed. A certain reserve is apparent in his music, though without any suppression of emotion. Among his anthems the robust vigour of *Glory and honour* and the eloquent intimacy of *This sanctuary of my soul* (entitled *Expectans expectavi*) have ensured their survival in the repertory. His setting of the *Passion according to St. Mark* was a notable rejection of all that was conventional and theatrical in earlier works of the kind.

THOMAS TERTIUS NOBLE (1867–1953) succeeded Harwood as organist of Ely Cathedral in 1892 and became organist of York Minster in 1892. In 1898 he left England and went to the United States as organist of St Thomas's, New York, where he spent the rest of his life. While still a student he wrote an Evening Service in B minor which was a model of simple and dignified expression – a nineteenth-century counterpart to Walmisley's Evening Service in D minor. He continued to compose throughout his life but never quite recaptured the innocence of his youth.

EPILOGUE

Tradition counts for a good deal in church music, partly because the liturgy does not change and partly because so much of the repertory is drawn from the past. For this reason church music tends to be less 'contemporary', in the fashionable sense of the word, than secular music written at the same time. There may be good practical reasons for this. Composers of serial music who venture into the world of the anthem and the service often have no personal experience of cathedral work and do not realize that their works create difficulties which are not easily solved by a choir which has to sing daily services. It is also arguable that music which presents too severe a challenge to the listener's ear is not entirely appropriate in an environment where what is heard should be an aid, not an obstacle, to devotion.

This is, however, no argument for a complacent conservatism. Much of the church music of the present century suffers from the facile acceptance of familiar formulas, which are generally presented in a competent form but are not illuminated by any spark of imagination. This music was often written by men who, whatever their interest in their contemporaries may have been, were not themselves of any significance as composers outside their organ lofts. Naturally the formulas did not remain unchanged. A self-conscious reaction against the mannerisms of nineteenth-century harmony, coupled with the rediscovery of English folksong, led to the glorification of flattened sevenths and the belief that 'modal' music was somehow healthier than anything written in the major or minor scales. The fact that both Vaughan Williams and Holst wrote masterly music in a modal idiom was naturally an encouragement to men of lesser talent. The result was a mass of superficially austere music which might be regarded as the perfect expression of muscular Christianity.

Tradition itself cannot be blamed for these weaknesses. There have been composers in the present century who, in following Stanford's lead, have not been content slavishly to copy his language. EDWARD CUTHBERT BAIRSTOW (1874–1946), organist of York Minster from 1913 till his death, WILLIAM HENRY HARRIS (b. 1883), organist successively of New College and Christ Church, Oxford, and St George's Chapel, Windsor, and HAROLD EDWIN DARKE (b. 1888), for 50 years organist of St Michael's, Cornhill, have all written church music which, though traditional in idiom, is neither impersonal nor smug. But it is above all in the work of HERBERT HOWELLS (b. 1892), a pupil of Stanford, that one can see most clearly how tradition can become the groundwork for the expression of individual ideas. Howells's church music, and particularly his services, is marked by the fastidiousness which he learned from his master. The very simplicity of the music is often deceptive. The flavour of it is neither old nor new but rather something peculiar to Howells himself.

Tradition reaches far back into the past. It is evident in the music of RALPH VAUGHAN WILLIAMS (1872–1958), who, like Holst, was sensitive to the music of the sixteenth century and at the same time had a sincere admiration for Parry, in whose memory he composed his *Prayer to the Father of Heaven*, on a text by John Skelton. He too valued simplicity. His little anthem *O taste and see*, written at the end of his life for the coronation of Elizabeth II, is innocent of any 'contemporary' gestures and at the same time a model of what church music can be if it is created by a simple-minded man. Sixteenth-century music has also exerted a strong influence on EDMUND RUBBRA (b. 1901), a pupil of Holst and a university lecturer at Oxford from 1947 to 1968. His *Missa Cantuariensis*, an English setting of the Holy Communion service, written for Canterbury Cathedral, spans the centuries with complete assurance and impressive effect. The energy created by a wiry polyphony is evident also in the work of KENNETH LEIGHTON (b. 1929).

The composers who are best known in the concert room have

contributed relatively little to the cathedral service. Notable
among these limited offerings is the *Magnificat* and *Nunc dimittis* by MICHAEL TIPPETT (b. 1905), written for St John's
College, Cambridge. This is remarkable as evidence that post-
war harmonies present no difficulties to a choir if the melodic
lines are singable. It also demonstrates the value of economy in
writing for the organ. This is a lesson that less gifted composers
might take to heart. Too many of them fail to realize that the
fewer notes there are in an organ accompaniment the more
effective it will be. The practice of writing massive organ parts
derives to some extent from Walton's *Belshazzar's Feast*, which
not only impressed the audience which first heard it in 1931
but has also had a powerful influence on a good deal of music
written since. There has been, particularly in recent years, a
spate of anthems of a festal character, the composers of which
have been tempted by a natural exuberance to batter the gates
of heaven and assault the ears of the congregation.

The problem of communicating with young people who
find the church services old-fashioned has not gone unnoticed.
Attempts have been made to attract them by writing 'folk'
Masses in an allegedly 'pop' idiom and music which is accompanied by a jazz ensemble. These attempts are sincere and
well-intentioned, but the music of this kind that has so far been
produced is neither distinguished nor stimulating. A further
drawback is the fact that 'pop' music is by its nature ephemeral:
the idioms change from year to year, and what was once
up-to-date rapidly becomes as old-fashioned as the more conventional music of the Church. There is a still larger problem
that has to be faced, and that is the language of the liturgy. The
advantage of using Latin in the Roman Church was, and still
is, that it is ageless. But the idioms of English have changed
since the time of James I, and expressions that were once
normal have come to sound artificial. Already the *New English
Bible* is widely used for the reading of the Second Lesson. Since
the New Testament is the source of three of the canticles –
Benedictus, *Magnificat* and *Nunc dimittis* – it would be logical to
argue that the new version should be sung as well as read. This
would not necessarily mean that older settings would have to

s

be abandoned, since the texts could be adapted, just as Latin motets have been adapted for English use from the seventeenth century onwards. But it would present a new challenge to twentieth-century composers, who might find in setting the language of our own time that it is not sufficient to be 'reverent' if the result is merely dull.

If the sung cathedral service eventually disappears, as gloomy prophets have foretold, a good deal will have been lost. Masterpieces which were designed for a particular purpose will be relegated to recitals, where they may impress as music but, deprived of their context, will lose much of their significance. It is clear, however, that mere respect for past achievements will not save church music from extinction. Its survival depends on a re-creation at the hands of composers who combine devotion to their task with an awareness of the world in which we live.

INDEX OF MUSIC EXAMPLES

GENERAL INDEX

s*